Also By Jason Youngblood

How To Get Money For College As A High School Student

Available on Amazon.com And Kindle

LIFE IS EASY, LIFE IS GOOD!

LIVING WITH AN
ECSTATIC LOVE FOR LIFE

JASON YOUNGBLOOD

Introduction

Throughout my life I have thought and said beliefs that have become themes during negative experiences such as "Life is hard", "Life's a bitch", and even the overstated "Why Me." Whenever I believe and profess these, I definitely experience life being hard and confusing. I often struggle with situations that are extremely hard to handle and I am miserably confused about the purpose of these negative situations. I believe that this experience is a direct result of my negative declarations and beliefs that "Life is hard" and asking "Why Me" during negative experiences.

Through my own self-reflection, I have identified six general negative sayings and beliefs that I believe and state during negative situations. You can identify for yourself any negative statements you say to yourself in negative situations. The easiest way to identify what are our subconscious negative beliefs is to listen to the voice in our head during the next negative situation. If we pay close enough attention we will notice that we feel a specific negative emotion and also say to ourselves these negative statements that are a means to vent how we feel about each negative instance. However, **as we notice these negative statements it is also of extreme importance to know that they are indeed self-fulfilling prophecies and are the sole reason we fail to fully love our lives.** I know this because **the moment I began adjusting my own negative beliefs, is the moment Life became effortlessly easy and amazingly good.** As a result of this self-discovery I wish to share my personal negative beliefs and declarations with you so that you can better identify your own and be able to adjust them in order to fully love your life.

My six negative beliefs:

- "Life is hard."
- "Why Me?"
- "Nothing good ever happens to me."
- "Never Fails!"
- "Damned if I do and damned if I don't."
- "I knew it was too good to be true!"

Through my own personal soul searching and asking for a solution to my life problems, I have been inspired by six positive responses to my negative beliefs. These six positive responses that are the antidote to my negative experiences are also the titles of the chapters.

My six positive responses:

- Life is easy, Life is good!
- There's a purpose for everything that happens in my life.
- Everything works out in my favor.
- My life is a journey of love.
- I am effortlessly taken care of!
- Everything good is specifically designed for me to enjoy.

I have experienced many personal situations that call for me to exercise these positive responses in order to fully enjoy and love my life. I will share some of the personal situations from my own life throughout the book so that you can understand how changing our perspective about life is the key to loving life!

A Brief Disclaimer

I am not a theologian or any authority on religion or spirituality. Although I do have a background in studying hermeneutics and homiletics at a bible college, as well as some experience in Christian ministry, I am not claiming to be a trusted source on spirituality. I am merely writing from the perspective of my spiritual journey from being totally disappointed and frustrated with my life to a discovery of an effortless and overwhelming love of life. Therefore, I wrote this book solely to inspire others, who are also disappointed and frustrated with their own lives, to discover their very own effortless and overwhelming love of life.

This book is for everyone, meaning that my intention in writing this book is to relate the concept of spirituality in a way that all can understand. Spirituality is not relegated or limited to people who follow a certain faith or religion. Spirituality belongs to us all no matter the spiritual language we speak or whether we follow organized teachings. Spirituality is an open connection with where we come from. Therefore, this book is simply an attempt to make plain the connection we all have with the source of all life and communicate that in a language that reaches beyond the limited language of religious texts. For example, what many people of faith demand we call god is actually what can be better understood as the source of everything that exists. What many faiths may refer to as righteousness, peace, and joy may be better understood as self-love, knowing everything will turn out good, and enjoying life at all times.

The words I write and the way I express them are simply what I, as an individual, have experienced and not to be practiced or believed as something that is true for everyone. The purpose of my words is NOT to persuade anyone who does not hold the same spiritual beliefs as me into believing or practicing the ideas that I share. Some will be inspired by my words and others may even be offended but it is entirely up to you as the reader to decide if you agree or disagree. Therefore, I will do my best to say things in way that is universal and applies to all instead of speaking in absolutes that only apply to people who follow a certain faith.

Every single solitary human being deserves to be aware of their connection with the source of existence in way that is easiest for them to understand. With that being said, no matter where you are on your personal spiritual journey I hope to inspire you to love your life to the fullest degree possible. I only ask that if you strongly disagree with anything that is written that you keep in mind ONLY what inspires you and ignore what you do not agree with.

The source of everything that exists is most commonly referred to as god. I believe that this source of existence, no matter what we refer to it as, is the tour guide to all of our personal spiritual journeys. As you read, this universal spiritual tour guide may bring things to mind you should be aware of and the ultimate result will be that you better love your life. This spiritual tour guide may also give you the ability to adjust any false beliefs about your life and give you the ability to be open to a new response to life that will prove far more beneficial for you.

Throughout this book I replace the word "God", what many use to refer to our higher power, with the word "Life". It is my perspective that god is the essence of all of life, meaning that god is the unfolding of life itself. I use the word "Life" to speak about our connection and interaction with god in a language more relatable to everyone, outside of the confines of a religious following. Therefore, if you follow any religious practice, please feel free to *replace the word "Life", which I use, with "God" throughout the course of this book,* for your own understanding.

Before we begin or continue our personal spiritual journeys while reading this book, I want to ask you to say a simple self-affirmation or prayer. This spiritual affirmation will start the journey of realizing your life has been amazingly good and that life will be even more amazingly good from here on.

I am open to Life and ALL of the goodness that is **freely** available for me to daily experience.

I give Life permission to give me the ability to realize ALL of my blessings that lie within **every** daily experience; positive or negative.

I allow Life to give me the ability to **change the way I interpret my daily life experiences.**

I am willing to let Life **adjust what I believe** about *my* life, in order to create a more positive and enjoyable daily experience, for me and those around me.

I freely give Life permission to bring willingness to my heart and humility to my mind so that I may **see things in a different perspective, which allows me to fully love life.**

Thank you so much for participating in that with me! If you desire to simply love life more or experience life as amazingly and overwhelmingly good, then frequently saying any variation of these statements will open the way for this.

Chapter One
"Life is Easy, Life is Good!!!"

Life can be experienced either miserably negative or amazingly positive. I believe that which one we experience is solely determined by two things:

A. **What we believe about** our overall existence and daily experiences.

B. **How we respond to** our overall existence and daily experiences.

What we believe about and how we respond to our lives is a learned behavior most commonly acquired by how we are raised by our parents and caregivers in our homes and neighborhoods. As a result we subconsciously learn what to believe and how to emotionally and mentally respond to conflict in life from our most influential caregivers. The way we have observed our caregivers responding to negative situations is usually how we learn to address negative situations. For example, if my family is a yelling family whenever they are challenged by someone, I will grow to be a yeller when I am challenged. If my family members are chronic complainers about negative circumstances then I will grow to be a chronic complainer about negative circumstances.

We also learn subconscious negative habits from society and culture that we observe. We unconsciously memorize and mirror our sources of entertainment and popular culture. As youth we learn to mimic the trends and popular fads that we see our peers and celebrities portraying. As a result we subconsciously have learned to entertain ourselves with trends to escape our personal suffering, depression, and frustration with life. Many of us can get so interested in what is happening in the news, politics, and celebrity gossip in order to escape thinking about and properly addressing our own lives. The thought of actually dealing with our day to day problems scares and confuses us and as a solution we ignore our lives and become fixated on other people's lives seemingly more interesting than ours. So many precious human beings cannot even function to enjoy themselves without a screen in front of them, communicating on social media, or commenting on the most recent celebrity news and political issues. All the while **we are unaware that we are drowning out our true and genuine higher self, who is the solution that truly heals us from all negativity in our lives.**

Mimicking negative patterns from our family and escaping the negative with entertainment will always reproduce the negative in our life in a vicious cycle. So how can we end these seemingly never-ending cycles of negative situations in our lives once and for all?

In spite of learning this negative response myself, through soul searching and traveling my own spiritual journey I have come to discover the single greatest *thing* that has changed the way I personally experience life and caused me to ecstatically and overwhelming love my life!. So…what is this "thing" I refer to?

It is simply the theory that **we as humans have the unique ability to choose our own experiences and create our own world.** We are, in a sense, superheroes with the power to bring into existence *whatever* we intentionally or unintentionally choose. I call this a theory because most people do not believe or experience this on a conscious level and therefore do not accept it.

Whether you follow a particular faith or not, it is important to note that the most respected religions and scientists tell us we come from somewhere. While there is a great debate between the religions and scientists about how to refer to the source of existence, many of us have wondered about or have an opinion on, what that source is. Being aware that we all come from the same source, no matter our strong disagreements about it, is the beginning to truly loving the life we have been given to live. We disagree as to whether it is a male, supernatural, all-powerful, all-knowing entity that created everything on purpose or whether it is a random combustion of gases and molecules that accidentally created the universe and existence. In other words, while many of us disagree as to what to call the source of our existence, **no matter our differences on the matter we can all agree that we came from somewhere.** If we came from somewhere, **we all came from the same source no matter our different opinions** about the nature in which this source originated existence.

I really do not want to re-litigate the age old argument of creation versus evolution. My only goal in this point is to make us aware that everything and everyone, in all of the universe, have the same source or origin. For the sake of avoiding unnecessary dissention let's just refer to this source as our **spiritual parent.** How we experience life is not determined by what we refer to our source as, it only matters that we are here and we know our relation to the universal source.

As I stated, this is not the argument of believing in god versus believing in science, this goes beyond man-made arguments. This is simply realizing that all of existence throughout the universe originated from the same source. Atheists and scientists do not have one source and people of faith do not have another source. If all of us have the same source then the two relevant questions we must answer is what is our relation to this source and why do we exist?

Answering these two questions for myself and no longer from the advice of religious leaders or spiritual advisors, was the spark that ignited my journey into overwhelmingly loving my life. I believe that the question we must all stop and ask is what is the source of my existence?

This is not a religious question. This is not even a question that comes with any requirements of devotion. It is simply acknowledging that just as all electrical appliances have a current that make them come alive and function, that we too as human beings have a life giving current that animates us and causes us to be aware of our existence. We then can simply ask our inner selves the question, "What is it that is fueling my body of flesh and bones with animation and energy?" What is causing me to be aware of my existence, think, move, and speak? Well the simple answer would be our high powered brains. However, the essential question is what is fueling our brains with the energy that activates our lives?

If we look at a device such as a tablet or smart phone without a battery or an electrical charge it is dead and lifeless and does not function at all. All functional devices need an electrical charge to come alive and function. This too is how the entire vast universe functions, from the sun rising and setting, the wind blowing, the oceans streaming, and the foliage of the fields growing. We all are alive with the same source that causes us to exist and move with life. There is no teaching we need to follow to acknowledge this. Consider this Native American proverb in relation to the Christian scriptures of the Bible:

"It makes no difference as to the name of God, since love is the real god of all the world." – Apache Proverb

"…God is love. Whoever lives in love lives in god, and god in them." I John 4:16

With this in mind, let us take the next step in life becoming effortless easy and good for us by also acknowledging that we are naturally connected and intertwined with this source. The fact that we exist and are alive and have breath in our lungs is evidence that this source is constantly with us and an intimate part of who we are. I personally believe that we cannot be separated from our source or from god as religion teaches us. I primarily believe this because god is to us, what our breath is to our lungs and what oxygen, water, and sunlight is to the earth. If we cannot be separated from the Sun or even from our breath while we are residents of earth then we cannot be separated from the source of our personal lives.

Next, we must move one step closer to how we can fully enjoy and overwhelming love our lives by considering the questions of how and why we exist. I believe that **our lives are a gift from our source designed for us to enjoy to fullest**. For me, that is the resounding answer that I am constantly given after I asked the essential question of, "What's the point of it all?" Every one of us who is on a search for more out of life has to feel and hear this for ourselves and not just be inspired by it from reading a book or listening to an inspiring message. I believe this is truly why we are here experiencing our individual spiritual journeys on Earth, where we learn how to love from our personal experiences. We in turn learn how to love others by learning how to fully enjoy our lives and existence.

In order to truly experience life as a gift and therefore live life as easily good for us, we must dispel the myth that life is a curse and a struggle to be survived. In place of this myth we must open ourselves up to the possibility that our lives were personally hand-crafted and designed to be loved, cherished, treasured, and fully enjoyed as a gift to us. I liken this to savoring something delicious that we eat or even spending time with someone who we will not see again in a long time. We cherish, appreciate, and notice all of the lovely things that are occurring during those experiences to make it more pleasurable. Our very own lives is the most miraculous and awe-inspiring gift we can receive if we are aware that we exist for more than just to be born, survive life, and then die. I believe we are here to fall in love with our lives, with ourselves, and with each other as the human family.

How do we fall in love with ourselves and each other? We do this by living our lives by the same formula in which we were originated and that is through creation. When I say creation I am not so much referring to the story of creation about the biblical origin of the Heavens and Earth or Adam and Eve. I am speaking of the process of originating something new out of nothing. If the source from which we come from has the power to originate life and existence, then it is my claim that we too as its offspring bear the same exact DNA, energy, and ability to originate existence for ourselves. Again, whether you believe god created the world in seven days or the big bang started the process of evolution, we can all agree that the beginning of our origins is still a part of who we are. If we believe in creation, then we are created in god's likeness and also have his ability to create. If we believe in evolution then we bear that same creative energy in our human bodies. I believe that the start to loving our lives is knowing that we have the same ability of our source to originate and create for ourselves the life we are designed to live.

We must become aware of the idea that we bear and naturally exhibit the same characteristics of our spiritual parent just like we do physically from our biological parents. Therefore we can truly experience our own personal creation or big bang every single day by producing our own pleasurable experiences. Our personal experiences do not occur as pleasurable; however the point of our creative power that we hold is the ability to transform any and every experience into a pleasurable experience. **We can literally turn darkness into light, sadness into joy, worry into peace, and guilt into forgiveness! We are, in our true essence, masters of our own universe in our personal experiences.**

Since our sons and daughters inherit certain physical features and mannerisms from you and I, in the same way humanity and our source have the same spiritual DNA, characteristics, and qualities and share the same ingredients to existence. **Our lives and the universal force behind our lives are one in the same. It is key to be aware of this! Asking our higher power to make this plain to us is the first step to the truly amazingly good life.**

As a disclaimer, I will briefly say that I am not saying that you or I are the religious depiction of an all-powerful God who controls the universe and doles out eternal sentences to the living and the dead on judgment day. I am simply saying that, just as a son or daughter looks and behaves exactly like their mother, father, and distant ancestors and share the same bloodline and DNA, that we as humans share the same spirit with the source of all existence.

With that said, we now understand how we can create an amazingly easy and good life for ourselves with how we respond during negative situations. We create an easy life with how we interpret our life circumstances through our perspective during negative situations.

Like everyone else I learned to interpret and respond to life through my family and culture. What I learned from my family was to get upset, yell and scream, and overpower all opposition by being the loudest and more forceful participant.

What I learned from my culture was the increase of money equaled the absence of problems and to strive to escape struggle through being rich and famous.

I also learned from my crime infested neighborhood that surviving hard times meant being tough or "hard" and being more violent and heartless than any possible adversaries.

In the process of learning these responses to life, I came to strongly believe the phrase "the world is an evil place", which as a child I repeatedly heard from my family. I also strongly believed the phrase "Life is hard." One of my favorite rap songs is by a music artist by the name of Nas. The song is called "Life's a bitch and then you die" named after the popular saying that describes the all too common earthly experience of a bad life before death. So these are phrases I mentally regurgitated whenever I would experience or witness adversity in life… "The world is evil", "Life is hard", "Life's a bitch and then…well….you die". Well Damn! Is there any hope of enjoying what was originally intended to be a gift and a blessing?

All of my experiences reflected and confirmed my suspicions of life being meant to be difficult. I went through the seemingly endless cycle of good days that waned in comparison to the bad days filled with frustration, depression, and hopelessness. I was constantly experiencing rejection from people that I wanted acceptance from, I was habitually losing my temper and exploding in anger, and I was continually slipping into depressive thoughts and emotions. I didn't see any other options of living and mistakenly thought that there was no way out of the rat race. I literally believed what I assumed I knew for a fact, that good and evil are at war and that evil is winning because bad experiences and bad news far outweigh good experiences and good news.

This couldn't be it! That sounded so suspicious to me. I couldn't put my finger on it but I knew somehow I was missing something about what the point of life is and why we are all here. I had to know!

Not everyone desires to know this truth but the majority of people you and I may encounter, apathetically accepts the rat race of existing, suffering, succeeding or failing at chasing material happiness to pacify the suffering, and then dying. What a shame! But there is electrifying news! That is NOT the purpose of our lives here on earth!

The Amazingly Good Life:

We are born into this life experiencing pain, struggle, and frustration. We are then mentally trained to seek and desire worldly pleasure to pacify these negative things. Very early on we begin to learn the habit of desiring material resources to satisfy us. As adults these desires may look like money, sex, a secure job, a house, car, entertainment, personal goals etcetera.

I remember when the light came on for me in this regard. I was confused yet intrigued by the possibility of life being easy, as you may or may not be at this moment. I had been so automatically prone to go after "the American Dream" as the answers to my life problems. When the light began to come alive within me, I was being prompted by my spirit, what most people refer to as their conscience, that if I wanted to be truly happy, then to be open to the idea of *no longer desiring and seeking material success as "the good life"*.

At the time of this epiphany I was 25 years old and bouncing back and forth between having to live with my mother and then living with my sister because I did not know how to pay bills on my own. I was extremely depressed, had little to no self-confidence, and could not keep a job. Therefore, my personal definition of "the good life" was living on my own, going back and finishing college, getting a well-paying job working with inner-city youth, being able to live my dreams of writing for film, being happily married, raising two beautiful children, and retiring wealthy. For others it may be fast money, exciting and frequent sex, fame, fortune, and luxurious living.

Whatever it is for you personally, please take a few moments to consider how you define the good life for yourself personally. What would need to happen in order for you to be happy by your definition? Do you have it? Good.

Now, may I blow your mind for a moment? Take a few moments to imagine that you have each and every one of those things and any other things that you can possibly conjure up that will make your life absolutely and positively exhilarating. Take your time, close your eyes, visualize yourself living with all of those things, and feel as happy as you can as if it were so. Take a few minutes to do this and feel this before continuing reading.

Could you feel the satisfaction and fulfillment that is there if you had them all? Well, you may not believe it at the moment but; **you can be even happier than this**…without any of those things! How can this be???

I believe and have come to experience that true, genuine, and lasting happiness does not come by material things that can be gained and then taken away. Once you have acquired all of those things, if any of them were lost or stolen then you would experience disillusionment and suffering…Right? Then that is not **True** happiness. I have come to discover, through many trials and errors of frantically seeking these things yet still having that itching feeling of distress and dis-ease, that **True Happiness, which spiritual tradition calls Joy, comes from within us and not from anything that can be attained outside of us.**

As a result of our discovery of our innate and inherent ability to experience ecstatic, overwhelming, and enthusiastic joy, we can correspondingly effortlessly experience all of our dreams coming true! This, indeed, is what I mean by the amazingly easy and good life.

This brings me back to the theory that we as humans have the power to knowingly or unknowingly determine and bring into existence *whatever* we **intentionally** choose. So what will we choose through spiritual intention?

Think of the story of Aladdin. He acquires a lamp with a magical genie inside of it who offers him three wishes of whatever he chooses. What if, just what if, he thought to ask for the lifetime friendship of the genie, instead of a mere three material possessions. What I am suggesting is that you have the option of either having a limited amount of your material desires or you can have the source of all those desires. You can choose fast and easy money or financial security, an affirming relationship or an exotic sex life, and even fulfilling your personal career goals or living out all of your creative dreams and visions......OR you can experience the source of these and everything that exists in the universe, living and moving in and through your life as a constant conduit and collaborator in your life!

Life is a Blessing and a Gift!

I believe and have found that everything in life is indeed a gift that is *given*. I have truly discovered that life is so much easier when it is perceived and experienced as a given gift. So, instead of us bumping our heads to go our own way, we are able to ask for the happiness we seek and the willingness to adjust our lives in order to enjoy that happiness.

When I make the statement that *everything* in life is a gift that is intentionally given, that is precisely what I mean. The ability to wake up in the morning, to walk, to breathe air, to use our body in every single, solitary, minimal task our body performs, and even the invisible functions of all of our organs, cells, molecules, and DNA; all are not by chance but are consciously given to us from our life source. Your entire life is a miracle and is a gift from the source of everything that exists in the entire universe. That being the case, everything we are and do can flow with so much ease, grace, and naturalness as we learn to ask source to live through us in areas we struggle in as well areas we excel in.

The bottom line of this principle is that a gift is given, and the gift of our lives and everything we do in life can be given as an effortless gift from our source. **Our only role in this is to recognize and be open to receive everything as a gift as opposed to earning it.** We are then able to ask source for the ability to know that we are doing everything from the simplest of tasks, even as automatic as breathing, because it is purposely given as gift. We are then able to ask for the ability to be open and willing to let go of our personal agendas in life and our sense of self-reliance on earning happiness for ourselves.

Most of this strong sense of self-dependency may come from a place of feeling alone or not supported by the relationships we have in life. We may think that if we don't do it for ourselves then nobody else will. We then have self-made purposes to get what we can by any means that we can think of. I believe it is this way of living that drives the frustration we experience in life.

If life is a journey and our destination is happiness, we can look at our personal lives as the vehicles that are transporting our souls to our destination. Many of us are traveling in the wrong direction and may not even know the destination is happiness. However, if we ask our source to give us the ability to let go of the "wheel" and allow the universal tour guide to drive the vehicle of our lives as our chauffeur then our journey will always be paradise. We will most certainly not always be aware of the purpose of where we are along the way. We will wonder the common questions of passengers during trips: "where am I, are we there yet, and why are we here?" Yet, we can come to a place of trust and enjoyment as we no longer seek heaven or eternal happiness as the destination but recognize everything within the journey AS the heavenly experience of happiness.

Life is Easy!!!!

Several years ago while I was living with my older sister, we were having an introspective conversation about life. The contents of the dialogue were related to the fact that we had been sexual abused by our biological father and that she, as a result, had vivid and tormenting nightmares to this day. I, on the other hand, had repressed memories about the actual abuse but remembered the events surrounding it. I specifically remembered the counseling session in which I was given a black adult male doll and a black boy doll. I can remember using the dolls to play in a way that gave the professionals reason to believe my father had abused me. I had also told them that my name was not Jason, but that my name was "Maleeka", indicating I had developed a alter personality in order to shield myself from remembering the abuse.

My sister then started to expound on how the abuse had negatively affected her relationships with men and caused her to hate them. She had also felt uncomfortable around me and avoided close contact with me for a long time because I look and acted precisely as my father did. She then uttered something that, at the time, had become her life's mantra. She stared at me with intent and parted her lips to emphatically affirm that, "Life is hard!"

I verbally agreed with her yet gave her some positive feedback about how our negative life experiences do not define who we are or what is possible for us. However, at that time in my life, I had still held on to my belief that life was hard and we as humans are forced, through no fault of our own, to deal with it as it comes and to play with the cards we are dealt. I would later be enlightened to the fact that life is indeed easily and overwhelmingly good to us in spite of our false interpretation of negative events.

It is almost as if a dearly loved member of our family gave us a mansion, a luxury car, and a million dollars of disposable cash and at first we are overjoyed with the blessing that it is to our lives. We then begin to experience the headache and tedious, toiling responsibility of managing the upkeep of the momentous property, the expenses of maintaining the exquisite vehicle, and the proper budgeting of an excessive amount of money to make it last. To put it in simpler terms, it's like when we as kids get the puppy we always wanted and begged our parents for, as long as we walked it, fed it, and cleaned up after it. We are thrilled the day we get the puppy and have a blast playing with it, but curse and strike the dog the day it destroys the kitchen and defecates in our room. Life is like the cute puppy that is playful and makes us extremely happy as children but that we have to clean up after when it takes a big crap in our room. I know this statement is far from the analogy of the box of chocolates that we hear so often but I think it's more accurate and true to life. Therefore, life is like the greatest most exciting gift we can ever receive but the management on a day to day basis is what can ruin that elation.

My worldview first began to evolve from life being hard into life being easy while reading certain books about spirituality. I had read two books by Carlton Pearson entitled *The Gospel of Inclusion* and *God is not a Christian*. I also read *A New Earth* by Eckhart Tolle, a lesser known author by the name of Joel Goldsmith whose book is called *The Infinite Way*, and *The Secret* by Rhonda Byrne. Reading *The Secret* in turn led me to read *Happier than God* by Neale Donald Walsh.

These titles were my introduction to the idea that God, Life, Spirit, the Universe, Energy, or Love is not withholding or reluctant or hesitant towards us in any way, shape, or form. On the contrary, our creator is beaming with excitement and elated to care for us and express itself through our daily lives. This is the essence of the title of this book; that as opposed to seeing our creator as a punisher or judge who is hard to please and gives us lives that are hard to live, we can now see that our origin and purpose as it truly is; as easily enjoyable

There was a time that whenever I thought of God, I imagined a translucent figure who looked like the God painted by Michelangelo on the ceiling of the Sistine Chapel or the Anglo-Saxon Jesus I had seen in so many paintings. I heard a thundering and commanding voice of what sounded like a combination of my biological father, my step-father, and the character of God in the Charlton Heston film *The Ten Commandments*. I did experience occasional goose bumps in church services and moments of enlightenment in my personal devotions. However, along with that came an unbearable guilt and emptiness when I sinned, a lack of satisfaction when I so passionately prayed for god's will, and a tormenting fear of judgment day in the end times. Although this is the experience that I and of all too many people of faith have, my image of God was beginning to shift from one of anger, control, vagueness, and stinginess into an abundantly intimate spirit who was extremely benevolent and desired to give me all that I needed and wanted, even more so than I desired to have it.

If you are a parent, most likely the strongest desires you have towards your children is to give them all of the food, clothing, and wisdom that they need for success in life. You may, as most parents, thoroughly enjoy the light-heartedness of their childhood and hope they mature into happy, healthy, and responsible adults. If there was a direct gift you could give them to assure this outcome, would you not freely lavish it upon them in abundance? It is my assumption that if your son and daughter asked for a close relationship with you always, for your wisdom about life experiences, and your undying support in anything that would truly benefit them, then you would not hesitate to offer that in a more than transparent manner.

Will you take a moment to imagine the children in your life in their most innocent, adorable moments? Imagine them happily playing their favorite game as happy as can be. Now, if there was anything that you could give them to make their childhood more wonderful, enjoyable, secure, and nurturing, would you not freely give it to them without requirement?

If you can imagine that warm and loving feeling you get in your heart when you think of the children in your life. That is the feeling that Life, God, Love, or the Creative Spirit has towards you and everything that exists in the universe. In fact, it is this feeling to the infinite power that the Creator has towards you and your life. This is why I say that Life is easily good to us. The image I had of God as one who reluctantly gives and who we have to beg, pray, cry to, and please in order to receive his blessings is the total opposite of what I have since found to be true.

"Which of you, if your son asks for bread, will give him a stone? Or if he asks for a fish, will give him a snake? If you, then, though you are evil, know how to give good gifts to your children, how much more will your creator give good gifts to those who ask?" (Matthew 7:9-11)

So where is the breakdown? Why has this not been the experience of countless humans who have asked, prayed, pleaded, and sought God and yet live and die feeling disappointed, disillusioned, broken, and empty?

I believe it is because of three things. These things have been adjusted in my own life and as a result I find it much, much easier to love my life!

1. **An understanding that the creator and I are connected**

My perception of what life is, is directly related to my perception of who the creator is.

It has shifted away from one of an inferior being in comparison to an intangible entity who could only be connected with through dogma, piety, and ritual. My concept of that connection eventually grew into one of a loving parent and son. I have now come to currently understand the connection as the relationship of water to all living organisms or the oxygen in the air to earth. For me, Life or God is an all-consuming, permeating energy that is the source and the substance of all that exists.

2. **An understanding that Life is for me not against me**

From a very early age, being the son of a pastor and being raised in church, I was taught that I was born a sinner and that God would not be pleased with me unless I submitted to his will. With this image of God as a child, I approached my faith in God as one of striving to change his mind from displeasure to pleasure towards me.

Once I was aware that waiting until I pleased god in order to receive his blessings, and waiting for what I prayed for until it was his will was not the mandate, I then began to experience an effortless enjoyment of life. I understood that God desired for me to enjoy life more than I wanted to for myself and had freely lavished me with an inner wealth of all I could ever imagine or ask for!

As our minds and hearts are enlightened to the fact that Life exists to perfectly bless us with good things beyond belief, we will always experience Life as perfect and amazingly good!

3. **An understanding of cheerfully giving to others what I want for myself**

"So in everything, do to others what you would have them do to you; this sums up all of religion." (Matthew 7:12)

If we want to experience Life giving us all the good gifts that we can ever need or want, then it is essential to desire those good gifts for everyone and love our neighbor as ourselves. Anything we could ever imagine for ourselves to have in order to live the good life and be perfectly happy, especially unfolds in relation to our being able to desire that those who hurt and offend us to be as perfectly happy as we want to be. It is within this experience that "Life" or "God" is easy and not hard.

At the time of writing this chapter I experienced a situation at my job that gave me the opportunity to exercise cheerfully giving to others. I had performed a task incorrectly at work and asked one of my co-workers how to correct it. They told me how to do so, which I appreciated and corrected the problem. I then witnessed them speaking with my supervisor in her office with door closed. Moments later my supervisor approached me and asked me to make sure I did the task correctly next time.

Apparently my co-worker had told my supervisor that I had done the task incorrectly. In that moment I felt frustrated and betrayed that they had done so. I initially reacted by being cold towards them and avoiding them even when they spoke to me. Shortly after this occurrence, I felt prompted by Life to forgive the person and want good for them and let go of the negative feelings I was having towards them. Wow, this was a moment of truth. I struggled with it because I really did NOT want to do that. I wanted badly to show them that I didn't like them and would not let my guard down around them again.

However, Life helped me realize that I would be so much happier and it would be so much easier if I could let it go as if it never happened and want good for my co-worker. I internally agreed and asked for assistance from Life to let go of my desire for revenge and to be able to desire them to be as ecstatically happy as I want to be.

Ask and allow Life to give to you

How do these three things grow and unfold in our lives? It is not by mentally understanding and then attempting to practice them, as we have done so religiously. I experience failure and disappointment waiting thereafter every time I try to do good things to earn blessings. However, I experience a **vibrant connection with Life, blessings in life**, and **love for others** as I **ask our spiritual parent to bring the truth of "Life is easily good"** to mind so that I realize it, speak it, and appreciate it as the key to creating it in my life.

Please remember that when it comes to matters of spiritual maturity, the responsibility is not ours to obey and follow rituals. **Our only responsibility is to ask the spirit of Life to give us the ability to co-operate with it. This is how I have found everything in my life perfectly and effortlessly falling into place.** This is why I can now confidently declare that Life is easy as opposed to being hard and is a beautiful, nurturing spirit as opposed to being a "bitch".

We can now ask Life (God) to reveal its effortless goodness to us so that, instead of believing that Life is inherently hard, we can perceive and experience that Life is inherently good to us, everyone, and everything!

Chapter Two
"There is a purpose for Everything that happens in my life."

So many times I have personally thought and said of the human experience, "we are created, born on earth to human parents, cursed by Adam to sin, experience an endless cycle of struggle, and then are punished with eternal unbearable suffering". In this light, life is seemingly a miserable and tormenting experience that is forced upon us without choice. During negative experiences I have asked the creator many, many times, "What is the purpose of this?"

Most people ask the general question of **"Why Me"**
during circumstances with which we struggle. In other
words, **"I didn't choose this"**, **"why is this happening to
me"** etcetera, etcetera. Does any version of this
question sound familiar? I have personally
discovered something that has alleviated me from the
taunting and haunting of this burning question "why".

The question of "why" always indicates two things:

A confusion about the purpose of the situation AND

A lack of choice to change the situation

When it comes to personal situations that we
struggle with or suffer from, it is common for us to feel
these two aspects very deeply. We can think and feel
them so deeply that we believe that there is no other
possible option than confusion and slavery to this
fate. Therefore, we tend to only respond as if there is
no purpose for the challenging situation or that there
is not a path to know the purpose. We also tend to
only respond as if we are slaves to the negative
circumstance and have no choice or option to change

it. However, I truly believe that *it is not only possible for us to know the purpose behind many of the circumstances we experience, but it is something we can depend upon Life to bless us with in any given situation.*

Over the years of experiencing the same type of negative situation over and over again I have become suspicious that there is a reason for the repetition and a lesson to be learned. In response, I asked Life for wisdom of the purpose of the cycle when specific negative situations repeat. The purpose is revealed to me as a free gift soon after the fact so that I can respond differently when it happens again. There have also been times when I became aware of the purpose of a negative situation in the midst of the experience so that I can adjust my response and to create a positive outcome at that particular time.

In those moments of realization I learned to ask Life for a willingness to *trust there is answer and a purpose to all of my life circumstances*. Through asking for this awareness I have discovered that **the key to knowing the purpose of any negative situation** in order to change it is my *willingness to respond differently to create a more positive outcome*.

As a result of this realization, if I experience a negative situation, my initial response is still typically frustration. However, I have learned that before I go too far into frustration or depression, I curiously think to myself "wait a minute" and pause to ask Life to help me acknowledge that there is a purpose behind **every single circumstance** and to freely give me the wisdom and willingness to respond differently. I also come to understand the purpose may not be revealed until much later so that it is easier to choose a different perspective and response when the negative situation reoccurs.

Therefore, there are three options in knowing the purpose as we ask Life for them:

1. Life revealing the purpose to us as it unfolds

2. Life revealing the purpose to us soon after the situation

3. Life giving us the patience and acceptance during negative situations because we know we will be reminded of the purpose during similar future experiences.

It is very important to also ask Life for the discernment to recognize when we can know the purpose and when we can accept the situation to be willing to learn from it. This discernment occurs as we give Life permission to reveal one of the three options as we experience each negative situation.

One of my own life situations can shed some light on these three options during negative situations:

Knowing the purpose

I took guardianship of my niece when she was 15 years old. She had been getting into trouble with the law and rebelling against her parents. I feel extremely close to my niece and love her just as a father would his daughter. She and I share the same exact birthday 16 years apart and I have always longed to be a father-figure to her. Therefore, I was enthusiastic about her coming to live with me. During the time she lived with me it was an absolute struggle for her to co-operate with my way of doing things. I attempted to spend a lot of time with her, I gave her guidelines and expectations to uphold, and I disciplined her with consequences when she failed to co-operate. She had never consistently had this structure and rejected it very strongly. She was defiant, belligerent, and rebellious for the first 3 months. She then realized she had no choice but to try to co-operate because her only other option was not convenient for her. She began to study hard in school, check in with me when she was out with friends, call parents for me to speak with before she visited her friends, and did chores around the house. However, all of this came to a head when I came home and saw her getting out of the car with a boy and one of her female friends, without my permission to leave home.

I approached her about this and her response was sarcastic and defiant. I then reminded her that I had freely given her privileges and made sacrifices for her to be happy. She disrespectfully replied that I didn't have to take care of her anymore. I also reminded her that in order to live in my home she had to co-operate with my expectations and if not then she did not have to live with me. She angrily replied that she had somewhere else to live. I then gave her permission to live there at which time she walked away and packed her things.

Wow, I was angry and hurt. Once she left to stay with her female friend I went back and forth on whether I did the right thing by giving her the option to leave. She was 17 at the time and was determined to live as an adult. I felt I could not force her to co-operate with me and that she would only continue to flex her independence with me. I was very angry with her for how she acted and what she said to me. I was even more so worried that she may make bad decisions and would wind up being in a hurtful situation. Yet, I felt strongly that I had made the right choice because she would only learn how to be an adult through trial and error since she refused to listen and co-operate. This was all happening at the same time as the end of my romantic relationship. Therefore, I was experiencing some strong emotional upheaval to the point of frustration, depression, and loss of sleep.

During a spiritual counseling session known as Reiki, I felt the ability to first, forgive my niece and no longer hold her responsible for her offense against me. I felt a strong sense to allow her to grow up and mature outside of my control. I heard a voice within me say that I was not *fully* responsible for her success and well-being, that I had put unnecessary pressure on myself, and done all that I could do. Now I could trust that our Life Force would guide her to where she needs to be outside of my influence. I was able to begin letting go of my desire to control those situations and trust that everything would come together perfectly. Although I still had a challenging time continuing to trust that those situations would play out in my favor, it was much easier for me to do so. I found the ability to grow in that trust and not repeatedly obsess over the situation or relive the frustration. I knew that I could take my foot off the gas, let go of my agenda, and the situation would be so much better for me as I did so.

After the whirlwind of that situation, I finally paused to ask Life what the purpose of it all was. In that moment I felt in my heart that they were for me to learn to rest instead of working so hard to prove my manhood and responsibility. I began to be aware that because I am the youngest of my siblings and have had no consistent father-figure in my childhood, I had developed a deep sense of proving that I am worthy of approval to my family. I also perceived that my niece would be well taken care of outside of my desire to earn the approval of my family by proving I am responsible.

My niece and I have since reconnected now that she is a young adult and we are able to interact with affection. I am at peace about our relationship and am free to offer her provision with proper boundaries in order to teach her responsibility without that fear of being met with resistance. I know that even if she does choose her own way that I can experience that without the pain of offense and choose to forgive her by balancing compassion and wisdom in my response to her.

As you read this example from my own personal life I trust that you are inspired to **pause** during each negative situation you experience and confidently ask your higher power
to give you the ability to sense what is being revealed, for the ability to let go of your agenda, and to be

aware that there is a purpose in the situation you are currently facing.

The timing of what you are able to sense and perceive will vary but you can ask for patience and acceptance and trust that you will be aware of the greater purpose as you ask and are willing to let go of your agenda in the matter.

Creating a positive outcome

Once we ask Life for this clarity and cooperation, we are then able to respond differently to each challenging situation we face in life and create a positive outcome out of every seemingly negative situation.

One of the things that has really freed me from the deep-seeded frustration with life was letting go of the idea that I was born to suffer without my choice. I began to wonder if before we are born, we actually agree to live life on earth. What do I mean by "before we are born"? I believe that our soul, which animates us and is the energy that causes us to be alive and aware, always exists. I believe that our soul will continue to exist after our flesh decays. In what form will it exist outside of the human body? I do not know, since none of us can scientifically prove that we have been to the afterlife. Any details that religious stories give us of the afterlife in Heaven, Purgatory, and Hell are all speculative for me.

However, I do suspect that just because the old television stops coming on doesn't mean there is no electricity in the house. While the TV is old and no longer receives a charge, there is still electricity coming from the outlet. Therefore, when our physical frame stops functioning, I believe that the energy that gave our bodies life lives on. I also wonder that if our souls live on outside of our physical frame, then could it have existed in a different existence prior to embodying our physical frame in birth.

Now, I will admit that this is a merely theory of mine and by no means am I indicating that this can be scientifically proven. So I do admit that this is purely speculative as well. Yet, my belief in this idea has in actuality lifted the heavy burden of frustration that life used to be for me and gave me a light-hearted enjoyment of life. While I can argue the impossibility of the concept along with any skeptics, I cannot, however, argue with the blissful experience I have had as a result. So while I realize this idea of pre-human existence may sound confusing, please allow me to attempt to state it scientifically in order to possibly better understand it on a spiritual level.

Science defines matter as a solid, liquid, or gas that has mass and volume or takes up space. Matter makes up all physical objects that we see with the naked eye, which is made up of molecules that are held together by a gravitational force to form it. These molecules are made up of smaller parts of an organic group called atoms. These atoms have at their core even smaller parts. Beyond this point is an overall unifying force called energy.

According to Albert Einstein, science defines energy as **always existent, cannot be created or destroyed, but can only be changed from one form to another while its essence remains constant.**

Therefore, our human bodies are matter in the physical sense; however our core essence that makes us aware of our existence is energy or what we call the soul. Sure we are made up of a body, organs, and brain but **what makes us alive, what turns us from off to on, what animates us, what quickens us and makes us come alive?** Just as an electronic device or appliance is made up of many physical parts but you have to connect it to an electrical charge to make it run.

To test this idea of our electrical energy, try sitting still for a moment, if you will, and just notice your immediate environment. Be aware of what you're sitting on, what you're looking at, where you are, how you're feeling, what you're thinking, etcetera. **That ability to be aware is the animation, energy, electricity, fuel, spirit, essence, and force that makes you work and gives you the ability to experience your life.** Not only that, this same human electricity is always on and **never** turns off. When I say never that is precisely what I intend to say.

Unlike an inanimate object that stops working when the power that made it work is long gone, our human physical frame may expire but the source that animates us and makes us aware, lives on forever and is continually expressed in another form. And not only that, this same exact force that gives us life has **always** existed since before our physical birth and before the beginning of time and space. It was neither created and can never be destroyed. It is often times referred to as God, Krishna, Buddha,

Brahman, Intelligent Design, Spirit, Love, or Energy. However, it is my belief and opinion that these are all one and the same, just expressed in different forms and called different names.

If there is any reality to this idea, then we can add one more concept to it, in that we are not separate from this force and are included in its divine expression throughout the universe. This divine energy is not He, She, or It. It is more so We. Just as a sports team or co-workers of a company all equally contribute to a common goal, just as many body parts are necessary in order for the entire body* to function; the body of the divine is every human, every life, and everything being expressed through the life of this force. (*Genesis 1:26, *I Corinthians 12:12-26)

That being said, *what if,* as our animating selves, we were present before the beginning of time and space and before the beginning of physical life on earth. What if, in perfect unison with the source of all existence, we chose to visit earth in physical form, chose the way in which we would be born, chose our parents, our upbringing, our life experiences, our challenges, our gifts, our talents, our successes, our failures, and our lessons we would have to learn on earth. What if we choose these lessons that would serve as a gift to us and cause us to grow as divinity in earthly form? What if the eternal knowledge that we give to God was something we are also a part of in our pre-incarnate state and also had pre-knowledge of our lives and chose our earthly experiences in spirit?

The biblical scripture of Jeremiah 1:5 says "Before I formed you in your mother's womb, I knew you and set you apart..." This of course, in religious tradition, is God exercising His will for Jeremiah's life. However, this also speaks to a greater purpose. The speaker communicates in such a way as if Jeremiah was alive even before he was born to human parents. The **pre-human** Jeremiah was able to be known and given a purpose prior to taking material shape. It is merely my assumption that this is the case for all humans and living things. So who is the pre-human you and I?

This can further be explained for better understanding by using water as an illustration. Water often times is used as a metaphor for spirit in religious traditions. Just as the same exact body of water can be frozen, then melted back to its original state at room temperature, and even heated to boiling to become a gas, the same body of water remains constant in its essence as it is expressed through many forms. The water does change to fire, wood, or some other element. So too, our spirit, which animates our physical body, is currently being displayed in earthly form, yet may have existed and may have the ability to exist in other forms once our earthly form as a solid passes.

This theory of a metaphysical existence cannot be proven on a material level. As of now, we cannot go back in time and see ourselves in our pre-earthly state or transport into the future to witness our existence outside of our human life. The only way of proof, in this instance, is through personal experience. Therefore, we can test this theory in our day to day experiences and witness the outcome of its reality.

Our original true self

Through our pre-born selves we choose every single solitary experience that we are encountering in our post-birth human existence. *This is why we can know the purpose behind any given situation in life*

and why we can choose the ultimate result to be
positive although its inception may seem negative.

Everything that separates us through space and time is only a misguided false perception, an illusion, a mirage. All of human suffering **only** exists in the confines of time and space and we are able to elevate ourselves beyond time and space through awareness of our true existence as the energy that exists before and after our human experience.

I believe that we choose this life though our pre-human awareness of our entire human life unfolding and then co-operate in agreement with the source of existence to be able to benefit from every experience of our human lives. I purposely use the word benefit instead of "suffer" or "learn" from, because ALL of life is a blessing to be enjoyed, even the apparent negative experiences. That is in fact why we may have chosen the negative experiences for our human experience; in order to benefit us in the end.

This truth can be illustrated by the biblical scripture Romans 8:28 which affirms that "All things work together for good to them that love god…" The question is who is it that loves god or put another way, who co-operates with the source of all of existence? I believe that "loving god" is often misinterpreted as human piety in the form of religion. The very being that loves god is not initiated by our human personality through a conversion experience when we say a prayer or perform righteous deeds but it is the gift of experiencing love given to us from our source. The ability to experience this ecstatic love for our existence is shared by all of humanity. So each and every one of us can share in this promise of every experience working out for our benefit and evolving into a blessing.

We might then ask the question, "How do ALL experiences and instances result in my good?" I believe this is true because every single solitary human experience that we have has a three-fold purpose behind it:

1. We were aware of the experience before we were born

2. We agreed to experience it because we were also aware of the ultimate outcome

3. We knew that the overall result contributes to
    our eternal joy in human form and our overall
    divinity in our post human existence.

Being that we may have been aware of our entire earthly experience before being born, we now have the awe-inspiring advantage of acknowledging our pre-human knowledge of the outcome of any given negative situation. Therefore, we are more so able to adjust our reactions in the midst of them.

This, my friend, may seem like a fantasy. However, my uncommon assumption is that the very next time you experience a noticeable negative encounter, if you take a moment to press the pause button on the cruise control of your thoughts, acknowledge your pre-born energy that is the source of your existence, and ask for its awareness of the situation, that you will discover this ability to know that there is a purpose behind it. The ultimate result will be that you experience it as an enjoyable benefit to your life.

Once we experience this awareness of purpose, we then become aware of the fact that we do not have to resist and fight our negative experiences, yet we can co-operate with them. We can realize that we no longer have to be reduced to just waiting for the scraps of the next positive experience to make up for the overwhelming negative ones or to tide us over until the next positive situation randomly occurs. We are instead aware of our ability to choose a positive outcome in the midst of every single negative experience because **the sole purpose of all negativity is to produce positivity into our lives**. Our inherent inner awareness will bring this truth to our minds and confirm it as we experience any negativity.

I believe that many if not all of life's positive blessings have been produced because of prior negative experiences. This idea can be seen through the miracle of a child's birth. During the pregnancy and labor pains, the experience is excruciating and seemingly unbearable. However, the miraculous joy that emanates from the birth of the child is unspeakable and overwhelming.

We then are also able to pause and be truly appreciative for our positive situations as we experience them and be aware of the purpose behind them. The purpose may be an answer to a spiritual intention or prayer we have had, it may be the ultimate result of an earlier negative experience we have gone through, it may be a blessing to prepare us for a future situation we may encounter, or it may be a free gift to bless us just because. Either way we have the full ability to be aware of the purpose and use the knowledge of that purpose to choose to co-operate with it for an ultimate blessing within the experience.

With this newfound ability to be aware that our lives have true meaning and purpose in every negative situation and that we have full access to choose more beneficial outcomes, we can now live out the truth of **"There is a purpose for everything that happens in my life"** as opposed to the misconception of "why me?"

Whatever life experience you are currently encountering you also are empowered to contribute to the resolution of the situation into an ultimate blessing, no matter how negative it may be. I encourage you to replace your personal "why me" with the following self-affirmation or prayer, as you experience whatever situation you are presently in the midst of:

"I am experiencing this for a specific reason. This experience was chosen by divine intelligence and I fully agreed to it in my pre-human existence. The ultimate purpose of this experience is designed to result in my overall enjoyment in life. I now ask my higher power to easily bring to mind the purpose of this specific experience and guide me in my response to it, so that it results in a blessing for me to fully enjoy and freely share with those around me."

Chapter Three
"Everything Works Out In My Favor"

As I highlighted in the previous chapter, every single thing that happens to us in life has a purpose. With that being understood we can now realize that the purpose of every situation, especially the negative ones, is to benefit us and not harm us. This truth is illustrated by the biblical scripture Romans 8:28 which affirms that "ALL things (positive things AND negative things) work together for good to them that love god."

There was a time in my life where I deeply believed and stated that the negative situations I had experienced in life were nearly all bad and no possible good could ever come from them. Every single time I found myself in the midst of a negative situation, I felt as if there was little to no hope of it being resolved. The only things I could feel during those moments were anger, frustration, and depression. Therefore, I felt compelled to complain the problem away. I talked about how messed up the situation was and vented about how upset I was about it. I did this complaining and release of frustration not only verbally to my friends and family but even more destructively within my own thoughts. I mentally rehearsed what made me the most upset about the negative situation over and over. The more I thought about it, the more trapped I felt that I did not know how to change the situation. Since I couldn't change the situation I might as well bitch and moan about it to help me feel better about it, right?

My belief that the situation was meant to harm me multiplied each time I found myself in a frustrating circumstance. I have since come to know and experience that all of the negative situations I have ever experienced have worked out to my absolute benefit and enjoyment in life.

All Of Life Is A Seed

One of the key illustrations that has guided me in the truth of this universal principle is the process a seed takes to grow into a plant. A seed is seemingly small and insignificant when you look at it but beyond the naked eye it has the power within it to grow and mature into a great and beneficial harvest when cared for properly.

Think about your greatest need you have in your life at this very moment. Now imagine that you have a very wealthy relative whom you can ask to meet that need. They overwhelmingly respond with enthusiastic willingness and assure you that they are going to take care of everything without any requirement on your part. This is hysterical news to you and you maybe are expecting a large check made out to you or maybe for them to make some calls and have it resolved. However, to your dismay when you meet with them to receive what was promised, all they hand you is a small seed.

You think there is some magic to the seed so you try to eat the seed like food, spend the seed like money, or even befriend and talk to the seed. You soon thereafter realize that the seed is useless, discard it, and view the whole experience as negative. You now realize your relative, although wealthy, is severely deranged and misled you to believe that a seed could meet your need. This would be frustrating to say the least. However, what you didn't realize at the time is that if you were to take that seed and bury it in the ground and nurture it, the solution to your need would grow out of that seed into a great benefit for you.

"Very truly I tell you, unless a kernel of wheat falls to the ground and dies, it remains only a single seed. But if it dies, it produces many seeds." (John 12:24)

This biblical scripture is confirming that whenever we choose a preferred blessing through prayer or meditation we are asking for "**many seeds**". Yet the only way to receive this blessing is that we are first given **one seed** that has to be buried in the ground. Now the ground is dark and imprisoning, yet this is the necessary environment for the one seed to produce our greatest blessing. All we are doing when we seek a spiritual blessing from Life is asking for the one seed, not the actual fruit or delivery of the blessing. When Life delivers the one seed it is through a negative experience and we feel as if our life is underground, dark, and trapped. This is the seed of our lives being buried in the ground so that what we desire will be produced.

This is one of the two keys that our prayers are able to easily come into our lives. In light of this illustration we can realize that whatever negative experience we are facing right now is merely our seed being buried into the ground. During this process we are to remain thankful that the seed is indeed producing and bringing to life all that is within it as a harvest to be received. To only see ourselves in the state of darkness and imprisonment after we seek a spiritual blessing would be as foolish as a farmer holding a seed in their hands and never planting it because the soil is dark and constricting.

Since the answer to our prayers, solution to our life's challenges, and benefit to our well-being often comes to us most commonly in the form of a seed, the only problem that remains is not in the lack of provision from God or Life, but in our lack of understanding to recognize the blessing that comes to us in the disguise of a seed. This is precisely why my spiritual intent or prayer has divinely evolved from begging an impersonal and intangible deity to change my negative situation, into asking the universal spirit of love, compassion, and empathy to **grant me the ability to change the way I see the situation and perceive it as a blessing in disguise**. This is because more often than not, the blessing I so desperately seek is already present in the form of the seemingly negative experience. Therefore **the negative experience we desire to change or that we are praying about is indeed an answer to a previous prayer we have had**. Asking NOT for our negative situations to change, but asking for our perspective to change is the second of the two ways that our prayers unfold easily into our lives.

How can this be? How can we pray for a blessing and get a curse and this be from god or the source of all existence? I will attempt to answer this question with another question. Have you ever noticed the very same negative experience that caused you emotional pain in the past over time turned out to be a good thing that caused you great joy? This may have happened several times in your life and you have simply not been able to notice the evolution of the bad experience into a good experience. It is my belief that every good experience begins in its seed form, which is a bad or challenging experience. In order to enjoy and be blessed with anything good, many times it must first come in the form of something we deem as bad or challenging. Now please do not let this concept discourage or frighten you. Although that may sound alarming, it is in all actuality the greatest news we can hear and take advantage of once we become aware of it.

The Law Of Opposites

One of my favorite hip hop songs is by the rap artist 50 Cent whose real name is Curtis Jackson. You may or may not have heard of him being that not everyone reading these words listens to hip hop. His song entitled "Many Men" is about his real life experience of being shot 9 times and nearly dying.

Whenever I listen to this song I am always inspired by the lyrics in the second verse:

"Sunny days wouldn't be special if it wasn't for rain. Joy wouldn't feel so good if it wasn't for pain."

Now although, within the context of the song he is speaking of being shot in retaliation of his criminal activity, the very words Mr. Jackson uses to motivate himself to come out of nearly dying, rings truth to the issue at hand. We simply cannot enjoy the sun without first experiencing rain. We simply cannot truly enjoy life without first experiencing pain. Life has revealed to me through many life lessons that this is why when I seek joy I receive pain soon thereafter, when I seek peace I find myself in a worrisome situation, when I seek a free and clear conscious I experience guilt and shame first. Just as in the scientific chemistry of the earth, the sun cannot exist without the moon and light cannot exist without darkness, so is the spiritual chemistry of our lives in that all the good things we desire and seek through spiritual intention and prayer cannot come into our lives without the seemingly negative things being given to us first.

This concept of receiving the opposite of what we desire, pray for, and spiritually intend is better explained in the book *Happier Than God* by Neale Donald Walsch. I would like to share this concept with you by discussing the author's words in detail. The author calls this concept I am speaking of "Inadvertent Selection of The Law of Opposites" saying "...the moment you choose anything – any outcome, object, or experience – the *exact opposite* of that will come into your life in some way." He goes on to say that "It is *necessary* for the "opposite" of whatever you are choosing..." to come to you first. Here, the word opposite is in quotations because the author indicates that we are actually receiving what we prayed for in the disguise of a negative situation. So the opposite of the blessing we seek is in actuality the precise answer to our prayer. In my own life I have discovered that receiving the opposite of what I spiritually intend is because it is the natural evolution of all good things that I desire.

I will now quote the author Neale Donald Walsch directly because reading his words were my first introduction to the awareness of this principle. I also desire you to read them yourself so that you can more fully understand why "negative" situations occurring in your life is actually a blessing and many times the precise answer to your prayers. The author states that:

> Because not many people know this, they can easily turn negative in their thinking just when the universe was preparing to place before them all their hearts desired. They do not see the appearance of the opposite as a sure sign that they are on the right path, heading toward their chosen objective. Rather, they see it as an obstacle, a blockage.
>
> They experience themselves to be up against the wall, when really they are standing in front of a doorway. Only *discernment* would allow them to know the difference. This is where the Gift of Wisdom comes in
>
> …If you see the opposite not as opportunity but as opposition, you will see it not as something that empowers you, but as something that takes power away from you. You will fall into negative thinking, not understanding that you, yourself, have used the Energy of Attraction to draw to you darkness as *well* as the light in order to *fully experience* the positive outcomes that you are creating.

What are we to do, then, when the Law of Opposites seems to be thwarting, rather than supporting, Personal Creation? *Understand exactly what is going on.*

Endeavor to see the appearance of the "opposite" as your first indication that Personal Creation is working flawlessly...Do not resist the opposite of anything that you wish to experience. Instead embrace it...

What you resist, persists. That is because, by your continued attention to it in a negative way, you continue to place it there...By focusing angry or frustrated energy on it, you actually give it more life.

Do not *fight* that which is opposite to your stated desire or your preferred outcome. Rather, relax into it.

I know that may sound strange, but I promise you, it works. Do not become rigid and tense, ready for a *battle. Never oppose that which opposes you.* Do not OPpose, COMpose.

...Come from a place of relaxed assurance that life is functioning perfectly. Yet do not confuse relaxation with acceptance.

"Resist not evil" does not mean that you should not try to change what it is that you do not choose...Change is not resistance, but alteration. To modify is not to resist, but rather, to continue Personal Creation.

I will now seek to give you a practical guide that will illustrate how to compose instead of opposing the opposite of what we seek through my own personal experience with this idea.

Four years prior to the writing of this chapter my older sister who was 33 at the time, had a bilateral stroke on both sides of her brain. The stroke was caused by an undetected tumor in her heart that eventually burst, with the blood stream causing near fatal brain damage. She was immediately unconscious and was not able to breathe on her own. She was life-flighted to the Cleveland Clinic and hooked up to a respirator that breathed for her. They also had her in a medically induced coma until she was able to breathe on her own.

All of the left side of her brain and approximately 75 % of the right side of her brain was damaged. My heart broke on the day the nurses informed the family that my sister would never be able to talk or walk again and would be a vegetable in a nursing home at best. The news was unbearable. All I could think about was how my sister had struggled to overcome the sexual abuse she experienced as a child and lived a challenging adult life of a difficult marriage, financial debt, and severe illness. She had overworked herself into a highly stressed state which caused her to develop Pott's disease and battle several seizures leading up to the stroke. I also thought about her children, my 15 year old niece as well as my 14, 2, and 1 year old nephews. I wondered how they were going to mentally and emotionally handle this tragic situation and if they would develop any severely dysfunctional habits as a result.

I had the difficult tasks of informing my 15 year old niece, whom I had guardianship of at the time, that her mother would never walk or talk again. I was not sure when the right moment would be or how to word it but I nervously told her during a severe snow storm while we were driving to the hotel we were staying in 20 miles away from the hospital. The moment I told her what had happened she burst into tears and called out "mommy". She and I were both devastated as I struggled to drive in a snow storm, hug her, and wipe tears from my eyes to see the road.

The following night while I was in the hotel room alone I was spiritually mediating on the tragic situation and did not know whether I should have the audacity to believe a miracle was possible or intellectually accept the situation and say my goodbyes. The doctor had told our family to make a decision on whether to keep her alive or let her pass. We were also informed that if we kept her alive she would always need nursing home assistance in a vegetable like state.

As I spiritually considered all of these things and asked Life for guidance as to the correct response, I experienced a moment of clarity and enlightenment. I felt a clear prompting that all of **this was happening for an intended purpose and that out of this seemingly very tragic and awful event would come the greatest blessing our family could possibly receive.** I did not know if that would mean she would be physically whole again or if her death would bring us closer together as a family but I knew that all was well no matter the outcome. I was at peace that this was an answer to my sister's many, many prayers.

The more I processed what had happened the more I knew that it was also the direct result of our family's prayers to fix my sister's broken marriage, sick body, and her financial debt. In that spiritually inspired state I realized that the direct opposite of our prayers was occurring first through this tragedy so that all of those things we prayed for concerning my sister could come about.

My mother would go on to tell the doctors to keep my sister alive and connected to the respirator. She strongly believed that she would breath on her own again, be taken out of the medically induced coma, and be conscious again. As the weeks passed my sister would squeeze the hand of visitors who spoke to her in her coma. At one amazing moment, when her daughter and I called to have the phone put to her ear, my sister raised her hand high into the air when she heard our voices.

Soon thereafter she had fully awakened from her coma, was speaking, and entered into physical therapy to learn how to walk again. Each time the neurologists would scan her brain the MRI still showed it as severely damaged. They informed us that it was impossible for her to be talking, walking and functioning with a brain with that degree of damage. We were also informed that the tumors that caused the stroke and needed to be removed with open heart surgery were now miraculously completely gone.

It has been four years since this incident and she is now walking and talking on her own and functions as much as she did prior to the stroke. My mother, brother in law, and teenage niece were the ones who were primarily making sure she took her medication and got physical assistance walking and maintaining her daily hygiene during the first couple of years of recovery. She is now able to live without the support of physical assistance and just moved into her own house.

In addition to her physical blessing, my sister's very painful marriage relationship is currently being resolved in the very best way possible. While my sister and brother-in-law are now separated, they both moved to the same city and co-parent my now 5 and 7 year old nephews very well. They get along much better as friends and co-parents than as husband and wife.

This is the most defining experience in my life that illustrates for me the principle of everything, including seemingly horrible experiences, working together with good things for my overall benefit and well-being. As we prayed for my sister's marriage to be fixed and her sickness to be healed the exact opposite happened when she nearly died. However, out of that experience all of the answers to those prayers came flowing in and are still unfolding as I write this to you ☺

Therefore, I say to you my beloved friend and sibling in spirit….that you do not have to misperceive the negative experiences in your life as "all bad" or only meant to be hurtful to your life. Remember that every single solitary experience you have has a purpose to, in the end, bless you beyond what you can imagine at this time and grow to be a source of overflowing ecstatic joy in your life. So instead of thinking or saying "nothing good ever happens to me" when you encounter any negative experiences, ask the Source of your life and the reason you exist to graciously grant you the remembrance that ALL things have a good purpose behind them, grow into a benefit to you, and will ultimately end up being the greatest blessing you could ever receive.

Chapter Four
"My Life is a Journey of Love"

In between our countless life experiences from our physical entrance on earth and exit from earth, it is exceedingly more than possible to reach the destination of enjoyment in life. This experience of enjoying life as the ultimate destination is what many in religious traditions call the "Promise Land" or heaven on earth. The biblical scripture of Romans 14:17 describes heaven on earth as feeling really good about ourselves even when we make wrong decisions, knowing that the negative things in our lives will easily work out in our favor, and fully enjoying life in even in depressing situations.

Many of us who grew up in a faith background are living with the mission of surviving suffering in life because going to heaven when we die will be worth it. Those of us who hold this belief often quote that ... "the sufferings of this present life are not worthy to be compared to the glory that we will see later". Some of us may even believe that the joys of heaven can be experienced on earth and often quote the prayer... "Your kingdom come, your will be done, on earth as it is in heaven."

No matter what your belief is about heaven, as far as whether it exists, who gets to go, and what it will be like, we can all agree that heaven is intended to represent a thrilling blissful experience. This ability to live a thrilling blissful experience is what I mean by "The Promised Land" when it is mentioned throughout the remainder of this chapter.

While I do not follow biblical principles exclusively, instead pulling my greatest life's lessons from many texts and experiences, I believe one of the clearest examples of how to fully enjoy our lives is found in the Judeo Christian scriptures. My tendency to quote Christian scriptures as illustrations is primarily based on the fact that I was taught to apply bible stories as a guide to my personal life from the time I was born into early adulthood. Be that as it may, I would like to share with you a story that has a great lesson of how we can love our lives in the most superlative of ways possible, which is to the fullest extent!

The term "Promised Land" is derived from the biblical story of Moses leading the people of Israel from enslavement in Egypt to freedom in Canaan. Canaan is the land that the people of Israel believed was guaranteed for them to live on as a right. This story is told in the Book of Numbers chapter 13. The account goes as follows:

As the people of Israel escaped slavery they traveled through the grueling desert for 40 years to reach "The Promised Land" of Canaan. Canaan was a symbol of escaping a life of suffering and enjoying life to the fullest. It would have been the equivalent of African slaves traveling the Underground Railroad from the South towards Canada or a Northern Free

State. When the people of Israel finally approach Canaan Moses sends 12 spies to explore the land prior to entering and report on:

- Whether the people who currently lived in it were strong or weak
- Whether it had many or few people that lived there
- Whether the people were friendly or not
- Whether the cities were open or protected with walls
- Whether the land had a lot of fertile crops or not
- Whether the land had trees or not
- And lastly, he told them to bring back fruit from the land in order to sample how good the land was.

The spies explored the land for 40 days and returned only to report that the Land indeed was abundantly "flowing with milk and honey". In other words, stating that the land had plenty of sumptuous sweet fruit trees to eat from and plenty of livestock to drink rich nourishing milk from. Therefore, it was a land where they would be well taken care of and they would possess, what I assume, was the main symbol of wealth in the time they lived in. There was only one problem;

- The people who currently occupied the land were not friendly and inviting
- The people were powerful and not easy to defeat
- The cities were surrounded by walls and not easy to invade
- And the worst part of all was the people that lived there were towering GIANTS!

Isn't this the common story of human life on earth? For the average human, we desire and strive for our vision of success in life but any personal success that exists always comes with giants, or personal fears we must overcome to enjoy that success. We must then answer the critical question that will determine how successful at life we will be. The question we must ask is:

What am I afraid of or **what is the main thing stopping me from enjoying my life to the fullest?**

Once we are truly made aware of what this is in our own lives then we will not only know that enjoying life is possible but we will be able to experience thrilling inner excitement in our lives.

I believe reaching our personal "Promised Land" or **discovering how to be thrilled with our lives is our main mission in life.** In fact, I believe that this is why we are here on earth. **We are here to find out just how amazingly thrilling life is designed to be for all of us.** However, there is always a struggle to achieve this because our interior psychological battles and exterior challenging situations oppose us from fully enjoying our lives. Many financially wealthy people have NOT had the extreme pleasure of experiencing this love of life because ecstatically loving life has NOTHING to do with outer wealth. Loving life is instead what I define as a wealthy inner life, which is the ability to experience love, peace, and enjoyment in any situation, especially in those that appear to be overwhelmingly negative.

You see my friend, the fact of the matter is that our lives are truly amazing. In other words, "The Land is good and flowing with milk and honey", meaning it is possible for our lives to be fulfilling and refreshing.

Life only seems challenging or difficult to bear because of the "GIANTS" or overwhelmingly negative life experiences that, invoke an inner fear to live our highest, happiest, healthiest lives, and causes disunity with our fellow spiritual siblings of the human race. We fear what we perceive as insurmountable suffering in our lives and in the world around us and then make our best efforts to cope with that suffering. As a result we do not enter the "Promised Land" of the ecstatic love of life.

So how then should we respond to negative life experiences, personal anguish, and suffering in the world that we fear we can never overcome? We can look at the remainder of the story of the people of Israel's mission to enter the Promised Land for an awareness of how to respond to *suffering in our lives* which is referred to as "*GIANTS in the land*" in the story.

Defeat Your Giants

Aaron, who was Moses' brother, responds to the spies' fearful report about the giants and says, "Let's go and **use all of our power and everything**

available to us to take possession of the land that is rightfully ours because we will no doubt overwhelmingly be successful!"

The question we must ask ourselves when facing suffering in our lives is: "What is within my power and available to me to be successful in the face of the overwhelmingly negative?"

Then the people who explored the land responded to Aaron and said, "**We are not able to go up against the people of the land because they are too strong for us**... the people that we saw living there are giants, so that **we seem as insects compared to them.**"

The next question we should ask during suffering is: "How do I view myself or feel about myself when I face an overwhelming problem? Do I feel defeated or hopeful that all is well?"

Then in Numbers chapter 14 the people of Israel cried loudly together saying, "We should have died in slavery in Egypt. We should have died while we were traveling through the desert. Why would god tell us to come and fight for this land, only to be killed by the sword? **We would rather return to slavery** in

Egypt. Let's appoint a leader who will take us back to being slaves in Egypt."

Finally, if we feel defeated by the negative we can ask ourselves: "Am I willing to change the way I look at the situation so that I can change the situation from negative to beneficial in your life or Do I want to keep doing the same things I've always done to manage my pain and stay in slavery to experiencing the same problems?"

Lastly, Joshua and Caleb, who were among those that spied the land, responded to the people of Israel saying, "The land we explored was extremely good and plentiful. ...*Do not be afraid of the giants in the land, which is very good to live in, because* **they (the giants) will be like food that we devour. Their shadow of protection has been removed from them so that we can do damage to them** as a people, because god is with us we should not be even a little fearful of them."

While I do not recommend any nation physically invading and stealing any other people's land and resources, the principle in this story remains true. How to successfully respond whenever we are faced with personal suffering or a mentally frustrating challenge is taught in this biblical story.

Many of the giants of negative experiences that we suffer from cause us to feel afraid to exercise the necessary principles that will produce what is actually good for us. We feel like our problems are unsolvable and far stronger than we are able to bear, and at times we may even feel as if it would be better if we weren't even alive than to suffer from fear of the negative. I know I have felt like life was so much to cope with that it would be better if I weren't even alive than to experience such emotional pain. As a result we would rather complain about the negative and remain in the slavery of it repeating, than allow our worldview about life and therefore our problems to be changed. When we feel this deep devastation we can be aware of everything that is available to us to fully enjoy life and find inspiration in the paraphrased words of Joshua and Caleb if they were to speak plainly to us today:

"Life is designed to be overwhelmingly good to us. Just the fact that we exist and have breath in our lungs lets us know that life is a gift that is to be thoroughly enjoyed (a land flowing with milk and honey). Therefore, when you experience suffering in this life (giants) that merely appears to be too much to bear, do not be fooled by its fearful and momentous appearance. Do not see yourself as helpless, hopeless, or as the inferior victim. Instead **see yourself as the far superior champion because all negativity is given to us for our eventual enjoyment!** Take courage that if the Source of life granted you the gift of human existence then your life is supposed to be overwhelmingly pleasurable. So any negative experience that would cause us to be discouraged will be as easy to overcome as devouring food when we're starving. We then know that there is literally no degree of negative circumstance that can stop us from enjoying our lives and we can choose to replace our fear of the negative with knowing that ecstatically loving life is rightfully ours to experience."

In light of these inspiring words from Joshua and Caleb let us recognize all of the things that are available to us to be overwhelmingly successful when we face the giants of our life problems.

1. Recognize that the Promised Land is rightfully yours meaning that life is designed to be overwhelmingly pleasurable.

2. Do not fear any giants that block you from your promise of loving life meaning do not see yourself as inferior to your biggest life problems but visualize them being easily resolved, as easy as killing an insect or eating food when you are starving.

3. Do not wish to remain in slavery rather than be free to love your life meaning do not be afraid to change your perspective about life and learn to think and speak differently about the negative so that you can be free from repeating problems you can't control. The number one way to see a resolution to any life problem is to not complain. Complaining will cause the negative to remain but a genuine feeling of thankfulness for the things that appear

negative will heal the problems into being a benefit to us.

Speak To The Rock

Not only does this story give us a lesson on how to respond to negative experiences that seem to defeat us, two other passages about the story teach us how NOT to react during negative experiences. One account tells us the improper reaction of Moses that kept him from entering the "Promised Land" or the ability to ecstatically love life on earth. In the biblical scripture of Numbers chapter 20, the people of Israel continue to complain about having to leave slavery in Egypt only to have to travel through the desert and not have enough sweet food to eat and water to drink. In other words, they were complaining about the negative experiences of the lack of nourishment and refreshment in their lives. They would have rather kept experiencing the problems they faced in slavery than change the way they thought in order to receive their promise of enjoyment.

In response Moses hears a divine voice within him and is instructed to **speak to a rock designated to** bring forth water from it for the people to drink. Moses reacts out of extreme frustration with the people for constantly complaining and **hits the rock with his large wooden stick.** Moses then hears the divine inner voice say to him, "because you did not completely follow what I instructed you to do, you will not enjoy the "promised land".

Here is another applicable lesson from this story on how to "enter the promised land" or ecstatically love life on earth. **Don't resort to attacking the rocks of negative situations with anger and complaining, instead we are able to speak to the rocks that block us from being refreshed in life.** We have the superpower to **speak our desired outcomes for negative situations into positive experiences.**

If we pay attention to Moses' improper response we see that his frustration with his life experience caused him to **lash out in anger and strike what was meant to be nourishment** to him and the people. Instead, Moses was **instructed to speak** to the rock out of a love for the people, so that water would be provided to the extremely dehydrated people in the desert. The rocks that seem to block our blessings, emotionally dehydrate us, and keep us drained of all energy, although they are seemingly hard to overcome, can be transformed into a more enjoyable resource through the power of our words. This is the same lesson Jesus taught in the biblical scripture of Matthew 17:20 when he says "because you have only a little trust, I am telling you that even if you had trust the size of a small seed, it would be more than possible for you to say to a mountain move from here to there and it will move, in fact, nothing will be impossible for you!" What this means is that the rocks and mountains that block us from progressing in life can literally be moved out of our way with the power of our words. This happens when we don't complain about our problems but thankfully express all of the good things that are present in spite of the problem and confidently state how we would prefer our problems to be resolved.

Therefore, the principle is do not strike your problems by complaining in anger about the negative. Instead we can speak the resolution of our problems into existence with the power of our words. Although this ability seems ridiculous, **I encourage you to say out loud the positive outcome you prefer in the midst**

of your current negative situation that seems impossible to escape.

What is the lesson we can learn from the story of Moses when we are frustrated and angry enough to hate our life experiences and curse the offensive people that Life has placed in our lives? It is simply that the "wilderness" is the common experience of human suffering on earth and there appears to be not enough of what we need to fully love life. Like the people of Israel, we are constantly searching for more in order to make our lives better. When we encounter negative experiences that cause us to feel defeated in our own eyes, we can enjoy life or "enter the promised land" if we take courage that enjoying life is rightfully ours. If our existence is designed to be a gift from the source of existence, then nothing negative can keep us from fully enjoying what is meant for us to enjoy. The words we use when we speak to others about our problems and words we mentally tell ourselves will determine if we can escape suffering and enter into fully enjoying life. Therefore we can respond by using the creative power of our words to speak to rocks or move mountains in order to fully enjoy any experience in our lives.

This is precisely the reason why we are given giants, rocks, and mountains…solely to witness and experience the miraculous enjoyment of their transformation into victories, refreshing water, and clear pathways. Instead of using negative words to curse our lives when we experience negative situations ("not again", "the story of my life"), we are empowered with the ability to declare how we prefer the situation to turn out and "…call those thing that do not exist for us as though they did" (Romans 4:17).

We can then speak to the negative situations in our life to change from negative to positive and be a luxurious benefit to us because we exist to love our human lives on earth. Wow! What a life-giving and freeing concept that we do not have to lay down and take negative life experiences, that we have the super human ability to fully love life in any negative situation.

Everyday Miracles

The other biblical text that continues the story of Moses and the people of Israel that teaches us how NOT to react to negative life experiences is the biblical scripture of Exodus chapter 16. This account of the same story goes on to tell us that the people of Israel continued grumbling against Moses and Aaron for leading them into the wilderness saying, "If only god had killed us while we were still slaves in Egypt, where at least we had plenty of meat and ate bread until we were full, because you have led us into the desert to kill all of us with hunger."

What a group! Here they were out of oppressive slavery and complained that there wasn't enough good food to eat while they were on their way to the Promised Land, which was exceedingly more enjoyable than Egypt. This was because every morning there was a miraculous appearance of a bread-like substance on that ground that they could eat. However, they were instructed to only eat as much as would last them for that day. When they attempted to save the extra food for the following day, the food spoiled. They had to eat this same bread-like food every day until they reached the Promised Land, where good food was more than enough to eat until they were full and still have left overs.

Now what I would like to bring to our attention from this account is that they proceeded to complain about what they were given as a miraculous gift. The supernatural blessing that they saw each day was not enough for them. Although they were experiencing what most of us experience in this life; just enough for what we need, they still were witnessing a miraculous gift that they complained about instead. The lesson here being that we often remain in the habitual thinking pattern of complaint about the miraculous blessings Source freely gives us. If we are blessed with a house or a car, then we find ourselves frustrated and complaining about the cost of the maintenance and repairs. If we have been blessed with a family, then we find ourselves frustrated and complaining about our spouse's short-comings and kid's disobedience. However what we fail to realize is if we continue this habit, then we will most likely bring about the experience of what I call negative life cycles.

Negative life cycles are illustrated in the story of Moses by telling us that they experienced the lack of enjoyment and fulfillment in life for *40 years* during what was only an *11 day* trip! Yes, you read correctly! They prolonged their miserable experience of extremely hot temperatures, dehydrating thirst, hunger pains, and just enough bread and water for a day from what was only supposed to take 11 days into 40 years of unnecessary suffering (Deut. 1: 2-3).

How could this possibly happen? How could the people of Israel have such a bad sense of direction that they got lost, back tracked, and walked around in circles for 40 years on an 11 day journey before they were able to enjoy life to the fullest possible extent? Prior to that they were barely getting by on scraps and could have arrived at their guaranteed, signed, sealed, and delivered promise of having more than enough and fully loving life. They remained in the seemingly miserable state of barely enjoying their life experience because they **failed to celebrate the bread-like substance, which mysteriously appeared every morning, as a miracle and instead complained that it wasn't enough.**

This is a valuable lesson I have recently learned in the last few years whenever I have asked Life why specific negative life experiences continued to cycle into my life for longer than they had to. As I meditated on the purpose of many negative situations that reoccurred in my life I was reminded of this biblical story and how it shows us how we get stuck in the same negative patterns of our own lives. **It is through the attitude of complaint that all negativity persists and even multiplies.** This is especially true in cases when we have miraculous blessings in our lives that we do not have the ability to notice and can only notice what there is to complain about. We can now see that complaint is one of the most self-inflicting decisions we can make in our lives. We sabotage our own miracles from unfolding in our lives when we pray for supernatural intervention about a situation and then complain about the process in which the prayer is being answered.

The people of Israel prayed for years to be delivered from the enslavement of the Egyptian King but when they had to walk through a desert for 11 days to do so, they complained about the miracles that they saw in the desert as not good enough. Today we do precisely the same thing when we fail to realize that the negative experiences we encounter after praying are actually part of the process to answering our prayers. Our only responsibility in the process is to know the negative experience is only temporary and part of the process and then **notice the "small" miracles that get us through the day and** celebrate them with joy instead of complaining they aren't good enough.

One of the simplest ways to celebrate the everyday miracles we miss and overlook is to ask for the ability to notice what the blessing is in the situations we complain about. This principle is also known as **"use what you have in your hand"** to perform miracles in your life. In other words if we want to transform any negative situation into a miracle we can notice what benefit lies within each negative situation for us and fully appreciate that fact instead of only being aware of how it is an inconvenience and complaining about it. We can better understand this through another illustration from the life of Moses in the biblical text of Exodus 4:1-9.

Use What You Have In Your Hand

When Moses is afraid to tell the Egyptian King to let the people of Israel go from slavery he is told to use what is in his hand to perform miracles in order to bring about that freedom. If we are going to be freed from the seemingly never ending cycle of negative situations in our lives that enslave us to frustration and depression about life **we also can use what we have in our hand to produce miracles that free us.** Using what we have in our hand simply means to not only be aware of what you do not have in your life and complain about it but ONLY be aware of what you have been blessed with that is seemingly an everyday mundane thing. If we learn to see as miracles the things we daily take for granted and have gotten used to, then we will live a life of the miraculous increasing in our lives. The apartment I live in, the car I drive, the relationships I have, the jobs I have, all have things about them that I can complain about but I am learning that they are miraculously provided to me for my full enjoyment and learning to appreciate and celebrate only how they benefit me instead of complaining about how they inconvenience me.

Many, many times, as I have gone through my individual life I have repeated and regurgitated the statement "This always happens to me" each time I encountered a negative experience that was similar or identical to a previous one. Have you ever noticed a negative pattern in your own life? For me it was something as simple as being clumsy. No matter what age or how mature I have become I still manage to trip over objects, run into walls, bang my head on sharp corners, and drop plates of food. As a child and teenager I would become very frustrated and curse at myself or the object with the declaration of; "Never Fails!", "Every time!", or "The story of my life!"

Each time I have an accident because of my clumsiness I deeply feel a disappointment with myself. In order to avoid "messing things up" again with my clumsiness and carelessness I criticize myself to stay on track and to be careful not to inadvertently break anything, hurt myself, or hurt others. Through this experience I learned very quickly to be obsessively *impatient* with myself as well as others in my life who did not meet my standards and impatience became a negative life cycle for me.

However, with my most recent examples of this anxious, crippling feeling of impatience with myself, I stopped to ask myself why this so frequently happens to me and why do I hate having to experience failure so fervently. As I pondered how to prevent experiencing this feeling from repeating in my life I gently began to feel that my experience of *gripping impatience with my personal failures* was for a designed purpose.

Another negative life cycle for me is that of a frantic fear of rejection. This reoccurring experience has repeatedly shown up in my life through the ending of friendships that I value and hold dear and rejection from the women with whom I sought romantic relationships. As I said to myself whenever I was taken over by impatience, I also habitually lamented the complaint of **"Not Again"** whenever I experienced rejection from people I frantically felt I needed approval from.

Now, on the surface I was merely attempting to show myself as a loyal friend or a dependable boyfriend. However, beneath the surface was a *breath-taking fear of rejection* that I was desperately trying to avoid by proving myself worthy to be loved forever. This experience has occurred frequently throughout my adult life. Every single occurrence of it has hurt me so very deeply and each and every single time it happens I have said to myself, **"Why does this keep happening to me?!"**

Each time these negative patterns reappeared though my life experiences, I resolved within my heart and mind that I was cursed; cursed because of my painful family history, and because there was something wrong with who I was due to damaging circumstances that were hopeless to repair.

If you, as the reader, are wondering the same exact question to your very own negative patterns or "life cycles" that seem to reoccur, they do not have to continue to vex your life. If you also notice that these reoccurring negative experiences produce feelings of hopelessness about preventing them from continuing to haunt your life, then please keep reading.

It is my humble belief that the source of our lives and everything that exists in the entire universe gives us these life cycles or reoccurring experiences as a means for us to learn the experience of endless and overflowing Love. This love we are meant to experience is an overwhelming love of ourselves, others, and everything our life offers to us no matter the circumstances in which those things arrive. You see whenever we pray for or spiritually desire anything to occur in our lives then it is imperative that we first experience the opposite of what we are praying for. So then whenever we are in the midst of a negative experience after it seems we have done all the right things we can take comfort in the fact that the negative experience is indeed a blessing in disguise and is bona-fide evidence that our prayer is being answered.

I truly believe that I was granted *rejection* and *impatience* from others as life cycles so that I could ultimately experience the blessing of *acceptance* through first being rejected and could experience the blessing of *patience* through first experiencing impatience. Therefore, my family, my life encounters, from the people I would meet, to the situations I would find myself in, would all be arranged to bring me the gifts, yes, the gifts of rejection and impatience so that they would ultimately bring me acceptance and patience, unconditional love and forgiveness.

This was the answer that was so freely and easily given to me once I directed my previously mentioned sincere question of "why does this keep happening to me" to the Source of my life. I simply voiced, "Since you are the one who created me and chose my life for me, can you reveal to me why I repeatedly experience these particular negative patterns?"

As you read this chapter you may be noticing some negative "life cycles" that frequently appear in your life which cause you to believe and repeat, "This always happens to me!" Maybe for you it is a reoccurring experience of not feeling good enough, anger, judging others, un-forgiveness, or loneliness that you do not enjoy living with. Whatever it may be, it can usually be identified as the same negative statement you make to yourself each time something similar occurs and leaves you feeling that you are destined to always repeat the same negative experience. It is essential for us to identify the specific statements and feelings we say and feel when we are in negative situations so that we are empowered to produce the opposite of the negative cycles they create.

The way to freedom from feeling entrapped by our negative circumstances we can't seem to ever get away from is to first notice the specific negative self-talk we say to ourselves when we feel negative. The next step would be to realize that **our negative self-talk is the culprit that is solely responsible for all the negative events that occur in our lives**. We must know that an end to our negative cycles is more than easily possible but **it is NOT dependent upon our desperate prayers to change our situation.**

Lastly, **it is necessary for us to feel and say the exact opposite of those specific negative statements and feelings we have in negative situations.** For instance, if a certain negative experience makes us feel like nobody loves us and we say to ourselves, "nobody loves me" or "good friends are hard to come by" then to break the cycle of that experience we must maintain a feeling of "I am adored and loved by my friends and family" especially the next time we feel betrayed.

When we find the courage to know that life is meant to be loved and when we have the audacity to speak positive experiences into existence in the face of negative ones we activate the principle that would have given Moses free access to the "Promised Land" of fully enjoying life.

To further illustrate the principle of celebrating the blessings that lie hidden in negative experiences we can consider the cycle of day and night as a perfect example. In order for the beauty and majesty of the stars to light up the sky of our lives, the Sun must first go down. Think of all the things that you enjoy about the night. For me, it is that I cannot sleep with light shining in my eyes, therefore in order to rest from the day the darkness allows me to close my eyes and hibernate for the night. It is also the beauty of the evening sky. There is nothing more beautiful to me that gazing up a full moon and a sky full of stars. I also enjoy the cool breeze that blows and replaces the blazing heat in the summer. Lastly, I love the city skyline of skyscrapers that light up against the black canvas of the evening sky. Just think that there are so many blessing brought to us through the evening and by the celestial beings that rule the night. While I love the day, I also love the night and recognize that I simply must accept the Sun going down in order to dance with the night and experience the gifts it brings each evening.

Therefore the very next time you find yourself saying to yourself, "This always happens…" in the midst of an unpleasant, undesired negative experience, ask Life and the Source of all things to gently remind you that the Sun of your life is simply going down so that you can experience the endless joys of the night. It may be that you experience rejection from a loved one such as I have experienced, but it is only to give you the gift of experiencing acceptance from the people that Life brings to you. You may be experiencing a reoccurring hurt from a past experience, but it is simply to give you freedom from guilt as well as the gift of forgiving those that have offended you. When we experience this we will find that the ability to do so is the absolute most exhilarating and thrilling experience we can ever imagine.

With this in mind I would like to let you know that each one of us has the secret privilege and ability to see beyond the apparent negativity in our life's circumstances. We have the unique gift of perception; perception of the pure joy that grows out of each situation that initially causes us frustration and anguish. So I welcome each one of us, including myself, to take courage when we face our giants, to ignore the fear of the outcome that would defeat us, and take courage and confidence in the outcome that will bless us and make our lives rich with enduring enjoyment in every situation. When we find this special ability to see between the lines and recognize that each negative situation is truly a blessing, we will see the inner complaint we have in our heads when we are frustrated with life begin to fade away. We will then begin to feel a great appreciation and overwhelming joy over the simplest of things.

So, as we move on to the next chapter, I invite you to first ask our spiritual parent to gently remind you that it IS NOT against you but enthusiastically in favor of you. Ask to be reminded that no matter how repeatedly negative your experiences appear to be that your life is specifically designed to be a journey towards Love; love of your very own life and the unconditional, un-requiring love of everyone you come in contact with.

I invite you to ask our spiritual parent to gently remind you that what appears to be the repetition of negative life cycles in your personal experiences can be complained about as "always happening" or they can be celebrated as a reoccurring message from Source because of its **ultimate purpose to bless us**.

I invite you to ask our spiritual parent to grant you the awareness that you have the distinct privilege of experiencing unconditional love of others, especially as you experience offense from them. Therefore, you will be able to experience the ecstatic love of your own life as you let go of being upset with them and want good for them.

Now, if you so choose, you can know that life is indeed a beautiful journey and the end result of all things you experience is not meant to curse you, it is designed, hand-picked, and tailor-made for you to absolutely love your life.

Chapter Five
"I Am Effortlessly Taken Care Of!"

Your life, my life, and the lives of everyone are meant to be effortless, easy, and automatic. Life can be as easy as breathing in the air, opening our eyes to see, listening to the sounds around us, reaching with our hands to touch, and opening our mouths to taste. Just as automatic as thinking thoughts and feeling emotions are to the human body, so too can the amazingly positive by-products of our grandest thoughts and feelings be overwhelmingly given to us without hesitation. That is how easy life is designed to be.

There are certain things in each of our lives that come automatic with little to no effort. We wake up, brush our teeth, bathe our bodies, and dress ourselves without second guessing ourselves and even noticing that we are doing so. In fact, the clearest illustration of what I mean is something most of us do every day. Driving is one of the most automatic things that you and I do and don't even notice the details. Have you ever been day dreaming or pondering something while driving and before you know it you had arrived at your destination? Now, the first time you may have driven to that same exact destination you may have carefully thought through the directions as you drove, making sure you followed every step. This is how the overwhelming majority of us live our lives; careful, strained, and full of effort. Yet, after traveling there several times, you were then able to drive there with no effort of thought whatsoever and enjoy the ride without stressing over getting lost. It is my humble conviction that this is how we are designed to live when it comes to enjoying the journey of life.

We Can Stop Repeating Negative Circumstances

I believe that the unfolding or resolving of life's circumstances happens in this precise manner as well, meaning they can be experienced automatically and with no effort. Initially, there may be strong mental resistance to this statement because of our common experience of desperately struggling to obtain what we desire out of life. Whenever we are mentally and emotionally wrestling with any negative situation we painfully labor through the encounter. We exert all of the physical energy we can muster in order to survive the experience through resistant prayer and attempt every single idea we have to change the situation to our desired outcome. Many times we may throw everything including the kitchen sink at the problem. So at the end of the experience we are so drained and sapped of energy, joy, and peace that we automatically fear having to relive or even think about the experience.

We may also tire of the stress and strain caused by previous emotional battles and simply throw our hands up, go about our everyday lives, seek escape through our own pleasurable coping mechanisms, and succumb to passively ignoring the issue for our own protection and comfort.

If we find ourselves doing either one or the other, we can rest assured that they are equally self-damaging responses to any and every life problem that we face. One the one hand, if you and I choose to mentally rack our brains and unleash negative emotions of stress and pressure in order to "fix" the problem, then we will find that we have simply rigged and manipulated the situation into a temporary state of convenience while failing to truly resolve the issue. This response will most likely cause us to be stressed, strained, depressed, and angry each time we encounter a similar situation as opposed to discovering an ability to better respond with a fulfilling trust that all is truly perfect and well in our lives and in every similar situation thereafter. This realization of emotional and mental stress will serve as evidence that we have not genuinely resolved any such previous issues, which is also why I believe the situation reoccurs and we respond in the same manner each time.

It took me a long time throughout my own personal life cycles to realize that the reoccurrence of similar negative situations plus the expression of the same negative response of complaint and frustration always equals the magnetic repetition of the negative situation. This is because expressing the same negative response of complaint and frustration feeds and gives energy to the negative situation to live again in the near future.

With the other possible response, you and I may choose to seek escape away from the negative situation and cling tighter onto our coping mechanisms or activities that give us pleasure so that we do not have to address the problem in any way, shape, or form. We may lend some effort of doing the bare minimum to survive the situation yet we resist attempting to apply the proper amount of effort in order to resolve the issue once and for all. We may choose this option so not to disrupt or cause any friction with any of the other involved parties because we cannot bear the thought of someone being upset with us due to something we did. Therefore, we seek to protect them and ourselves from any inconvenience.

We may also choose this option because of previous traumatic experiences that have stripped us of all ability to tolerate any ounce of struggle and has impregnated us with a gripping fear of defeat if we choose to fight the battle of resolving negative situations. This usually is fueled by a false image of prediction where we see the situation turning out worse. We fear that if we give any positive effort to resolve the issue than we will suffer grave disappointment due to the fact that we see the experience ending in the worst possible way to only result in our detriment.

I personally tend to habitually exercise the aforementioned option of meeting each negative situation with all of my mental effort to figure out and fix the problem I may be facing. I also have had personal relationships with people who habitually exercise the latter by avoiding struggle in order to protect others involved from offense and protect themselves from the harm of more emotional pain.

People who may be like me in my habitual response may internalize the stress and feel as if they are weighed down with responsibility. They may find it impossible to participate in activities that give them pleasure and rest. These same people might believe that they are more intelligent in their response by facing the problem and addressing it with all of the necessary brainstorming and problem solving until the situation is resolved. However, I invite all of those who may respond in this fashion to re-evaluate how they felt during the most recent occasion of that response to resolve a personal negative situation. In our evaluation we can honestly ask ourselves if we have experienced a more peaceful and effortless response whenever we encounter a similar negative situation that previously caused us to feel a negative emotion.

It is revealing to also ask ourselves if we feel pressured, explosive, and confused each time we face a challenging problem in our lives, then are we truly "solving" the problem with our typical response to the negative. I humbly propose to any such reader that if we produce the same negative emotions in each example of a personal challenge then we are not resolving the problem at all. I believe that the reason we experience the same negative emotions and seem to re-encounter negative circumstances that make us feel them, is because we have not resolved the **true issue at hand**.

Our goal on the surface may be to just get through the experience, survive it, or no longer experience it at the moment; all the while assuming that if we encounter the same situation, that it is inevitable that we struggle and wrestle with the resolution as we have always done.

I would like to present an alternative if I may. I invite all of us who face problems head on to consider that we can have a much more pleasurable experience with each situation and truly resolve our confusion, anger, and stress as opposed to postponing it to reoccur. We can do this by shifting our intention from merely *not* experiencing the negative situation to intending to receive a genuine feeling of fulfillment, enjoyment, and confidence that the situation is working out perfectly to our personal benefit in the midst of all negative experiences. As we open ourselves to the possibility of this and make this our main intention we will sense a more effortless and pleasurable response each time we face a negative challenge that previously caused a feeling of explosive pressure.

Seek To Heal Yourself, Not Change The Problem

Therefore, the true and genuine issue at hand is not to change or fix the *problem* but to change *us* so that we do not continue to negatively process problem situations. I have found for myself an overwhelming relief of unnecessary frustration during negative challenges in my life once I shifted my focus from changing the problem or situation to allowing myself to change, grow, and mature with each and every negative situation. I have had the pleasure of discovering that the true purpose of negative situations in our lives is to inspire change within us so that no matter how negative a situation is we are able to experience the same love of life we would have if we had just won a million dollars. To be ecstatic with joy in the midst of apparent tragedy would cause so much confusion and bewilderment not only for us but especially everyone around us. However, I would be remiss if I did not share with you this little known secret to **why we experience the negative…it is so that we can be changed into more love, not hatred for our lives.**

With that being said, I would like to offer a simple suggestion for those of you who may follow a religious tradition or pray to God when you face troubling circumstances. One of the easiest ways to see a negative situation unfold perfectly for you is to no longer focus on praying to change the situation into your preferred outcome. I have practiced this time and time again and have seen amazing solutions to the problems in my life when I have, instead of praying for the *problem* to be fixed, prayed for *my* eyes to be opened, for *me* to be changed, for *me* to grow, mature, and flourish in my love of life. I believe this is true because in our tendency towards selfishness as humans we truly believe that it is about fixing problems so that we can be happy when **it is really about "fixing" or healing us, not our problems.** We can truly feel as if we have no problems at all, no matter what seemingly negative situation appears in our lives, if we allow our focus to be shifted from fixing problems to healing ourselves so that we love life in all situations.

So the very next frustrating, stressful, or depressing situation you may find yourself in, try praying for yourself instead of for the problem. State that you are ready to receive overwhelming joy in all situations and **ask for a breathtaking love of life inside of yourself no matter what is happening on the outside.** Ask that you would **be willing to change and transform into your true self, which is love.** In every single negative situation from this moment on, ask not to change the situation, ask that your perspective about the problem would change and that you would grow in your thoughts and emotions until you think and feel as if the "problem" did not exist.

Now, those of us who may exercise the latter preference of "keeping the peace" or "playing it safe" as a subconscious habit may choose to escape by indulging in celebrity gossip, reality TV shows, browsing social networks, listening to music, or frequently going out to social events to dance and drink in order to cope with the stress that comes with our negative life issues. These same people may believe that we have a more pleasurable response in avoiding emotional pain and protecting ourselves. However, I invite all of those who may respond in this fashion to re-evaluate how they felt during the most recent occasion of that response to escape a personal negative situation. In our evaluation we can honestly ask ourselves if we have experienced a more peaceful and effortless response whenever we encounter a similar negative situation that previously caused us to feel a negative emotion.

It is revealing to also ask ourselves if we feel like escaping each time we face a challenging problem in our lives, then are we truly "solving" the problem with our typical response to the negative. I humbly propose to any such reader that if we produce the same negative emotions in each example of a personal challenge then we are not resolving the problem at all. As I stated about the previous response, I believe that the reason we experience the same negative emotions and seem to re-encounter negative circumstances that make us feel them, is because we have not resolved the **true issue at hand**.

Our goal on the surface may be to feel better about it, make it go away, or no longer experience it at the moment; all the while assuming that it is inevitable to continue to encounter the same situation and respond to it the way we always do.

I would like to present an alternative way if I may. I invite all of us who fear and avoid resolving self-conflict to consider that we can have a much more pleasurable experience with each situation and truly resolve our fear of disappointment and failure as opposed to postponing it to reoccur. We can do this by shifting our intention from preferring to ignore our true thoughts and feelings about negative situations to intending to receive a genuine feeling of fulfillment, enjoyment, and confidence that the situation is working out perfectly to our personal benefit in the midst of all negative experiences. As we open ourselves to the possibility of this and make this our main intention we will sense a more effortless and pleasurable response each time we face a challenge that previously caused a negative feeling.

We may experience a subconscious mistrust that there is no use in attempting to resolve the issue because we fear that because we don't know how to fix the problem we will just be disappointed by the problem remaining or reoccurring. However, instead of experiencing the repetition of these same beliefs we can now trust that we have a spiritual parent and source of life that is with us and that we are not in the conflict by ourselves. We can now trust that our source or spiritual parent passionately cares for us more than we care about ourselves and looks at our problems as easy fixes, even easier than killing an insect, even as easy as the easiest thing we can think of although our problems merely *appear* to be insurmountable to us.

Our spiritual parent knows precisely what to do in each and every situation we face, no matter how terrorizing it may be to us. If we trust that every single solitary thing we are concerned about, our source cares all the more about and is easily resolving it in accordance with our cooperation, we will then begin to experience our external problems and our negative internal response to them be mysteriously yet certainly resolved. We will then see less of the same problems reoccurring as we spiritually allow ourselves to respond to them with love, joy and peace instead of fear, stress, and anger. When this happens we will notice that we still love, thoroughly enjoy, and feel amazing about our lives even in the midst of apparent problems we used to melt down about.

How in God's name is this even possible? You may be wondering this question, as I did when this outrageous idea first entered my heart. It is only possible by one measure. It is possible when we allow ourselves to let go of our agenda for the problem, our outcome for the situation, and our preference for the circumstance. Each time I've genuinely acknowledged and entertained these radical ideas I've seen, what seems to be, the impossible occur.

Whenever I have come to realization that I am not dealing with a problem alone but with the intimate partnership of the most powerful force in all the universe is when I have always witnessed as an amazed by-stander, the magic of life unfold even better than I could have ever imagined. In that moment, I also realize that this all-powerful source of all that exists passionately cares about me personally even more than I care about myself and knows the number of hairs I have on my head, knows the number of breathes my lungs breathe, knows the number of beats my hearts makes, and intimately knows all of my concerns.

When I acknowledge that the seemingly impossible issue is bigger than I can handle in my human tactics and then allow myself to completely forfeit all of my solutions to fix the problem, is when I have always encountered a force powerful enough to easily resolve all of my life issues yet gentle enough to passionately nurture me as a loving parent.

What I am speaking of is not a religious experience by any means. It is an awakening and awareness that the universal source of all that exists is not too big to also be my life's source in every sense and with every detail. This awakening requires no conversion and requires no sinner's prayer, no personal devotion. This consciousness of our connection with our original source is merely a light switch that is turned on within us whenever we honestly ask for an openness and willingness to forfeit our life's independence and allow ourselves to be taken care of and loved by what only appears to be the unknown.

For me this unknown mysterious force is not an entity or being that dwells in another realm that we must access with spiritual exercise. For me this force of loving energy is within us and intrinsically apart of us. We need no rhyme or reason or ritual to access this force. I have been able to experience this force magically and wonderfully unfolding my life the more I have realized that this force of love is not a mystical being that needs to be accessed or is withholding being accessed. In fact, I believe we have had it backwards as a religious culture, all these centuries attempting to connect with god. It is not the source of existence that needs to be accessed; it is us that need to be accessed by the source of our existence. Therefore, we need not perform to connect with a higher power that is seemingly far superior to our seemingly inferior selves.

It is my personal experience that this force of love is not so much a being to be worshipped but a feeling of being highly regarded and adored as opposed to being a repulsive sinner. We must come to be fully aware of this very feeling and experience of being adored and treasured as an individual. This is what ancient scriptures mean when they tell us that god IS love. I believe the mystery is that god is not so much a being or personality but is literally the purest experience of being personally loved and cherished. When we allow ourselves to feel and experience this then we are truly connecting with our source and expressing our highest selves.

In this light when the resolutions of our problems do not play out as neatly as we have planned or thought; this is the time that truly matters because this is the time that most of us will panic. We desperately want to start taking matters into our own hands, calling in favors, taking out loans to pay the bills, complaining to our friends and family hoping that someone will be able to help us. We put up walls with the people who have hurt or offended us so that we don't allow them take advantage of us again. We do this because many times the situation appears to not be going anywhere or even worsen. This is when we can continue to pray not for the problem, but for ourselves to continue to feel amazing about our life and to be in love with life and take no thought for our concerns. In other words we do not have to have one single worry about any life situation and can relax and rest knowing that we "know people in high places" that is taking care of everything.

We Are Greater Than We Think

During the times that we subconsciously activate our preferred method of solving problems, we may do so because we believe that stressfully struggling and worrisome wrestling with our life issues is inevitable. Why, isn't this the way it has always been done since the beginning of time for humanity? The tendency and habit of our human brain is to immediately revert into "fight or flight" mode, where we either double down to take on the challenge with the intention to struggle to survive the situation or we pick up and evade the intensity of the struggle by avoiding the reality of the situation. When this happens we are entering the subconscious belief of **"Damned if I do, damned if I don't"**. In other words we are re-enforcing and re-telling ourselves that it doesn't matter if we try to respond the right way or respond the wrong way because the outcome will be the same negative situation either way.

This is an honest yet grave mistake that we as humans have been programmed to do. We hit repeat in our minds when we encounter the negative. We automatically respond the same way we always have and yet produce the same negative outcome. We subconsciously believe and exercise this very untrue yet wildly popular mindset of being inevitably doomed, cursed, or fated to be unevenly matched against the negative things that cause us unnecessary mental and emotional harm.

It is my spiritual intention to bust this myth and debunk this widespread invention of our mental propaganda so that we can experience freedom from the feeling of being cursed to defeat when we are faced with the so called negative or evil that seems to overpower our lives. My proposition is a simple yet bold claim:

You and I and designed to be champions in life. Not in the sense of a competition, a fight, or a war having a winner and a loser, but in the sense that there is literally no competition that can hold a candle to the powerful force that we are. Allow me to be more precise in directing my claims at the most common myths we as humans tell ourselves and keep us in the mental and emotional prison of the so called "negative". Consider the opposite of the negative myths we believe:

- Life is not created to be a struggle

- Evil is not winning the war of good versus evil

- There is no war between good and evil

- To live is not to suffer

- There is no "bad things happening to good people"

- There is no evil to overcome with good

- There are no problems to be solved

- There is not a war between angels and demons

- There is no Devil versus God

This is true because there are not two separate realms warring against each other therefore there is not a negative life and a good life. There is only a good life in actuality. Any other "negative" experience we have is an illusion, hallucination, and merely a reoccurring bad dream that we've been having and is not reality.

I believe these bolds claims because I have come to this amazing realization that the same energy that raises the Sun every morning and sets it every evening, that causes oxygen to permeate our environment on earth so that we can breathe air, that feeds the birds in the sky, and makes the foliage of the fields to grow is also flowing and permeating our individual lives. Whether you define this energy as God or Science, this same energy is not only the source of these miraculous constant occurrences on our planet; it's also the source of our personal lives. I believe this is true because on a spiritual level we are born of the same DNA of this source and on a scientific level we are made up of the same molecules and dust particles that all of the constellations throughout space and all of the elements on earth are made of.

If those bigger than life things occur without our effort, input, or agenda, then so it is in our individual lives, which is guided by the same force and energy. We are not able to influence whether the Sun rises or sets. We are not able to influence whether the wind blows or whether oxygen fills the air. We are not able to control whether or not the stars shine bright in the nights sky. Therefore, we are now able to realize and be aware of the Life behind our lives which occurs without our effort, input, or agenda.

We can be aware of our inherent ability to let go of our lives and allow the true source of our existence to unfold our individual lives in the same way that it unfolds the mysteries and wonders of the universe. We can do this because our molecules, atoms, and particles that form our bodies are the same precise molecules, atoms, and particles that form the ever expanding, never ending universe and the same spirit that gives us life, gives life to the vastness of the universe.

Therefore, you and I are as important as the Sun. We are as vital as the wind. And just as we need the sun, air, water, and the fruit of the field so does the universe need us. We are equally as powerful as the vastest galaxy in the entire universe! This being the case, we can now see our "problems" versus us, as laughable.

If an immature child gets upset with the brightness or heat of the Sun and attempts to hurt the Sun by throwing a rock at it, it is a laughable offense because the rock cannot even begin to reach the Sun. Even if the rock could somehow reach the Sun, the size of the rock is merely a speck of a speck and even invisible, compared to the Sun. Even if it were large enough to compare to the Sun, the power of the sun would consume the rock upon approaching the Sun's energy field. Imagine if the Sun were able to have human emotions. Would it be fearful of a child throwing rocks at it in a feeble attempt to injure it?

Humor me for a moment and image if the fear of the negative that we constantly live by when it comes to our individual lives were also prevalent when it comes to how we view the universe. Have you ever been afraid that when you go to bed at night that you would wake up without a Sun and encounter total darkness and total freezing? Have you ever waken up in the morning and feared that the Sun would come too close to the earth and burn it up in a single flame? Have you ever feared that when you gaze at the stars in the sky at night that they would begin to fall and strike the earth? Outside of Hollywood special effects this fear has not occurred to those of us who do not suffer from a severe and rare phobia. If we do not live by this ridiculous fear then we can rest assured that we no longer have to fear the "negative". We no longer have to fear life's "problems". We no longer have to fear "evil". We are not damned no matter what we do because there is no curse or negative fate that exists. I truly believe that all dark moments can evolve into ecstatic moments of joy and that life is meant to be loved.

How To Create A Miracle:

Finally, I would like to further illustrate this principle of being destined and designed for overwhelming joy in all experiences. We can know this not because we have an unyielding agenda and plan for our own lives and seek to make good things happen for us with our best efforts. We can know we are designed for overwhelming joy simply being that the universal spirit is also the source of our personal lives. There is a story that perfectly portrays this principle. Whether you believe that the origins of this story is a parable for illustrative purposes only or you believe that it literally occurred as an historical event, we can all learn from its overarching message. Without taking up too much page space and reading time, allow me to paraphrase it for us.

The biblical figure Abraham had a wife named Sarai who could not have children. They had a maid from Egypt whose name was Hagar. Sarai was so distraught that she could not have children of her own that she came to Abraham and said "Please go into my maid; perhaps I will obtain children through her." This can be read about in the biblical scripture Genesis 16.

Now Sarai was compelled to such an extreme solution because previously in Genesis 15:2-5, God spoke to Abraham and promised him he would have a child of his own, and not only that, his descendants would be as numerous as the stars of the sky. Therefore, Abraham and Sarai were so convinced they would have a child but were still not getting pregnant no matter how often they attempted to get pregnant, no matter how much they wanted to get pregnant, no matter how much time had passed.

Now can you imagine, you and your spouse have miraculously heard the voice of the Creator or the divinity of your personal faith, who promised that you would have a child even though you were infertile or barren? This was the situation at hand for Abraham and Sarai. They were desperately expecting to get pregnant after hearing from the divinity of their faith and still were not with child. Then Sarai thinks to herself that maybe god meant they would get pregnant some other way and suggests that her husband have intercourse with her maid Hagar in order for them to have a child.

If you are not familiar with this biblical story then you would not believe what occurs next. Abraham actually has sex with Hagar and she gets pregnant and has a boy who they name Ishmael, which means God hears. Then of course, since Hagar was able to get pregnant, Sarai becomes exceedingly jealous and begins to purposely mistreat her. Now guess how old Abraham was when he impregnated Hagar! He was a mere eighty six years old! Then when he finally impregnates Sarai he is

100 years old! When Sarai gives birth to the child they name him Isaac, which means **laughter.** The story then offers an explanation as to why there was such a long wait between the promise of a child and Sarai being able to get pregnant. (Genesis 21:2-7)

According to the writer of Genesis, the elongated wait between promise and fulfillment of the prophecy was so that Sarai would be well past the age of childbearing. Therefore the purpose of the wait was so that the **birth of their child would surely be a miracle and for everyone who was a witness to laugh at the impossibility** of giving birth when not only barren but also past the physical age. Therefore we can conclude that the moral of the story is that it was biologically and scientifically impossible for Abraham and Sarai to conceive children, and that was the purpose of the wait until they were too old. They surely lost confidence and became frustrated several times over with what they thought they were sure of and even desperately attempted to create for themselves.

This story reminds me time and time again of the outcome when we as human desperately attempt to create for ourselves what only our divine connection to the Universe can spiritually or miraculously produce. Whenever I find myself in an impossible situation, this story offers me so many truths that let me know how to properly respond in order to cooperate and hasten the manifestation of the miracle.

First, I am reminded that the circumstances surrounding all miracles are always physically, biologically, and scientifically impossible. So if we have been or are currently in such a negative situation, then we're in great company and are on the right track!

Second, when I know that I am promised enjoyment of life and do not experience that in any given situation, if I decide to take matters into my own hands and attempt to produce the desired result through my own personal agenda and preference I actually sabotage and am counterproductive to the miracle of loving life.

Third, when we find ourselves seemingly going backwards and our faithfulness in doing things "the right way" seems to produce no results and actually make things worse it is simply because the greater purpose may be to make the situation physically impossible so that when the miracle occurs, it is all the more laughable and enjoyable.

With this parable or example from a spiritually themed story, let us consider that whenever we feel as if it doesn't matter if we try to do the right thing because it always ends in nothing happening or things actually getting worse, we can know its only purpose is for us to experience the birth of **laughter in our lives**. Its only purpose is to transform the impossible to the indeed possible and add to our overwhelming enjoyment. For the very definition of a miracle is the unexpected, unpredictable, uncontrollable solution to a dire and impossible situation.

So, if I can relay a message from this story and the overall purpose of this chapter is don't try to fix your life problems yourself. Don't make a math problem or science project out of your life circumstances by trying to figure them out and understand them so that you can fix and solve them with your preferences. Instead, as a more enjoyable alternative, we can know that there is a greater purpose behind every "impossible" experience and trust that the overall outcome will be laughable for us and the people around us who witness the outcome. For that is always the purpose of our lives here on earth; to laugh and to make laugh.

Being Present

The simplest way I have found to allow the Universal Source of our lives to easily solve all "problems" we experience is to first ask for the ability to feel connected to our source and deeply feel the interwoven hook up we have with our originator. This is a type of meditation exercise that anyone can practice without religious rituals.

We all have the ability to acknowledge that vibrant feeling of connectedness we have with the creator in the midst of any negative situations big or small. We do this by simply allowing that feeling of connection to flow from the channel of our physical human body into the atmosphere or energy field of the physical space we live in. I am aware these three things are very elusive and mysterious; however, allow me to briefly put them in common terms to make it practical for you.

Whenever I am sitting still either in traffic in my car, waiting in line at the grocery store, at my desk at work, in private at my house, or basically whenever I am forced to wait for the busied action of my day to resume, I make it a point to acknowledge my ability to *feel alive*.

I notice that if I pay attention to how the energy in my skin feels that I can sense a slight vibration in my hands. This is the energy that is at the core of our human body. I then start to pay attention to that feeling of vibration in other body parts, my arms, my feet, and my head specifically. You may notice this slight vibration of the skin in other body parts as you are enabled to spiritually feel connected.

When I practiced Christianity as a religious tradition I referred to this experience as "feeling God's presence" or "feeling the Holy Spirit". This was primarily activated as a participant in a church service or practicing a spiritual ritual. However, as I have grown into a more universal spirituality that I believe applies to all humanity I have noticed that I am able to access this "feeling" anywhere and anytime. I just sit still and focus my attention on the vibration that exists in one body part and then continue to feel it gradually spread in other body parts as well. Then as I feel that vibration stronger and stronger, I envision it passing and flowing out from my body into the atmosphere, like a gentle breeze blowing throw my body and strengthening all the goodness I possess into a light that consumes any dark situations in my life and carries it into the world as an invisible force, like an electrical current giving life to an electronic device.

When we consciously feel the source that gives us life we are like an efficient appliance or device that operates with ease. Ignoring the feeling of our connection with our source is like that same device attempting to operate without any power. In the same sense when we live life without taking time to acknowledge and feel the current that gives us life we are grinding our gears without the needed power to operate with the efficiency and ease that we are to designed to function with.

I now refer to this experience as "Being Present". Being present is the best way to channel our higher selves and access our natural ability to heal our life "problems" that we previously worried about and desperately exhausted our limited resources to solve. While being present we now do not feel as if we have to solve our problems and instead feel as if they do not even exist and *become joyously oblivious to our so called "problems"*. We then find and witness those situations easily and effortlessly resolving themselves without our meddling or interference. It is then that we can experience our Universal Spirit, the very same that raises and sets the Sun and grows all the beautiful foliage of the earth, automatically and miraculously being the source of our lives. This automatic miraculous source of energy makes being alive easily enjoyable while effortlessly taking care of our lives as opposed to unsuccessfully struggling to change the events in our lives and being "Damned if we do, Damned if we don't".

Finally, I would like to give life to this principle of being "effortlessly taken care of" by exercising the power of our words and speaking it into existence so we can experience it working in our lives. Feel free to put this declaration in your own words or as a prayer to God to release the energy of effortless living into your very own inner enjoyment.

So, I now declare that we release our agenda, our preference, and our desire from our current negative situations.

We allow the same power and force that controls all the wonders of existence to unfold in our lives with the same care and compassion.

We trust and let go of our fear that we are cursed and damned to repeat frustration and depression.

We let go of the myth and false belief that we are doomed and fated to experience the "same shit, different day" or that we are "damned if we do, damned if we don't".

We acknowledge and accept that our spiritual parent will be the maestro of the song we call life and conduct a symphony of the most beautiful sounding chorus with all of the individual sounds of our experiences that by themselves are unpleasant but as a collective sound are beautiful, mesmerizing, and inspiring.

We trust that the current impossible negative situation is as much of a problem as a stone is a problem to the Sun and that our seemingly very real problems are merely a bad dream that we can awake from.

We now allow our spiritual parent to gently wake us from the illusion and hallucination of doubt and fear and grant us the ability to know our fate is overwhelming joy in every scenario because we know that the Universal Sprit that connects us all is the source of our lives.

Chapter Six
"Everything Good Is Specifically designed for me to enjoy!"

Have you ever been amazingly surprised by a positive experience that was what you've always secretly desired? Maybe you have been blindsided by a blessing that was so good that it made you feel suspicious that you didn't do anything "special" to deserve it? Possibly, you even had a string of "good luck" that was so out of the ordinary that you became extra cautious of your actions so that you didn't "jinx" it or mess anything up? I know I'll sound like a damn infomercial but …If you answered YES to these three revealing questions than you are probably like me in feeling like unexpected blessings are "Too Good to Be True".

Whenever I come into an extra amount of money, meet someone who is interesting that I just click with, have a challenging life situation miraculously work out, a problem a loved one is having is mysteriously solved, or if someone with influence does me a huge favor without me asking for it, I secretly feel that the "good luck" I am experiencing is "too good to be true".

What I mean by "too good to be true" is mistakenly being suspicious that the good things that unexpectedly happen to us are indeed temporary and if we are not careful, one false move could usher in the usual bad luck that occurs more frequently.

Although this response of being suspicious of good is as common and automatic as breathing, it is counterproductive to the truly ecstatic, seemingly lucky life that we desire; where everything falls into place for us and everything we touch turns to gold.

Here's one sure fire way to know if you are in this category of thinking unexpected positive experiences are "too good to be true". Simply answer this revealing question: Do you believe that you've experienced the bad and unlucky for so long that it has stripped you of your ability to even hope that anything good will happen to you?

If we answer yes to this, and believe me I have several times over, what has occurred is a string of bad luck has indeed been on auto loop for so long that we actually have to come to *expect and accept the bad AND became deathly suspicious of the good*. If this feeling sounds familiar, I assume that you, as the reader, can relate to my repetitive encounter with random luck that is seemingly insufficient in not lasting long enough or not occurring frequent enough to alter the bad karma of our lives.

Expect And Accept The Good

Expecting and accepting the bad flow in our lives and being suspicious of the good, as innocent and automatic as it seems, it creates a negative energy field, cloud, karma, and aura that permeates around us and prevents the flow of the "too good to be true" to operate in the same space. It is like a fortress or protective wall around and over us that **blocks good things that are constantly flowing in our direction from entering into our lives** for us to personally experience and enjoy. You see we want to live a life full of the "too good to be true" to the point where we can't keep count of all the "luck" we experience and it literally overlaps and one amazing experience doesn't end before another one comes and overtakes us.

We are indeed missing out on this life of overwhelming "luck" that is alive and well and pulsating to be released like a mighty waterfall into our lives and the lives of everyone and everything around us. I liken this experience of altering the karma of what we mistakenly refer to as "bad luck" into "good luck", to a dam breaking after years of mounting pressure from a massive body of water. Can you see the wall of the dam shattering and giving way to the rush of water that consumes everything in its path? This is what you and I are constantly on the brink of. Even now, and before you were even made aware of your truly great potential, we are constantly on the precipice of this overflow and freefall of good and awesome things rushing in and through our lives.

You and I can shift the flow of energy in our lives and open ourselves up to not only have these awesome, enjoyable experiences flowing in our direction but also into our personal experiences when we exercise three things.

First, when we personally experience this flow of goodness, it will be like when we have friends and family who always tell us about wonderful things that have happened to them and we secretly wish it would happen to us. We assume they are lucky and wonder why things like that never occur in our lives.

Hearing about good news happening around us is the Creator sending good things <u>in our direction</u>. We must understand that goodness is highly contagious and you and I can catch it very easily depending on our perception of what appears to be luck or chance for someone else. We catch it and personally experience this goodness by not only hearing about it but feeling fully appreciative that the Creator specifically hand-picked that experience for that person to enjoy and ecstatically rejoicing in their goodness as if it was also happening for us. Since we are all connected by the universal spirit **when we hear about something good happening to one of us it is happening to all of us who hear it and that is the universe trying to bring good things into our life as well.** When we hear about good news for anyone we can ecstatically rejoice in it because on a spiritual level it is happening for us too. Our genuine pleasure in the goodness in someone else's life is intimately connected to the goodness in our own life.

The moments we hear good news for others it is important not to secretly wish that it would happen to us too. For example, is we are single and someone we don't like lets us know they met someone and it was love at first sight, we must not secretly think, "I give it a week." We must be completely appreciative for the joy that has come into their lives and share their good feelings about their good news, especially for the people we don't like.

Second, after we are not disappointed that "nothing good" has happened to us and can rejoice in the goodness of others, we will then be able to notice good things in our own lives. **We will become amazingly aware of all the minor and mundane good** things that occur all the time in our lives that we miss, overlook, and take for granted. Once our eyes open and we are able to see every single good thing that occurs in our life from the most minor and mundane to the great and awesome things, we will see each and every good thing as custom designed by the Creator for our personal enjoyment. Then **when we view as amazing the things we have learned to take for granted, more amazing things will unfold for us that cause us to rejoice and enjoy life more.**

Lastly, when these unexpected blessings begin to increase in our lives it is essential not to respond by being suspicious of the good and subconsciously believe it is temporary. In the moments that we have unexpected goodness flow into our lives we must **respond by knowing that the experience was specifically hand-picked for us as a gift from our Creator.** We must also feel our worth and value that the Creator would think high enough of us to make us feel special. It is literally like being wildly in love with someone and always thinking of them and wanting to show them how special they are to you. This is how the Creator feels towards us. It is **constantly looking**

for ways to show us how special we are to it and how highly it thinks of us.

Even if one particular blessing is designed to be temporary does not mean it is too good to be true, it just means it was meant for a season and there are plenty of other blessings designed for us in their perfect time. Therefore, when a pleasurable experience does not last we must understand that it was only for a season. We must understand that there is an infinite and endless amount of goodness where that came from and expect amazing things to continue to constantly flow into lives.

To make this idea more plain and easy to understand I would like to give you a couple of personal examples of when life was "too good to be true" to me. These examples show how we can respond to unexpected luck the right way so that we do not "jinx" it but actually increase its flow into our lives.

When I first moved to Columbus, Ohio, the city I currently live in, I drove a 1989 Lincoln Towncar that was on its last few years. It had not been well taken care of and was a bitch to fill up with gas. I had just graduated from college and as a graduation gift my mother bought me a 1998 Honda Accord. It drove way better than the Towncar and was better on gas mileage to say the least. After a short while of enjoying this wonderful car the transmission went out and I would have to shift the gear into reverse to drive forward and vice versa because the gears were all backwards and messed up. Therefore I had to give up my graduation gift that I simply loved driving and that had replaced the lemon of a car I had before. In this moment, I thought that a good reliable vehicle was too good to be true and was anxious about the next car I would have to settle for.

I found a Buy Here Pay Here car lot that let me trade the Honda in for a 1990 Cadillac Deville. Now don't get me wrong I love Cadillacs, but I was not looking forward to the poor gas mileage that came with it. On top of the abysmal gas mileage, I soon came to realize that the car had an electrical problem that caused the battery to go dead just about every time I turned the car off. I had to ask for a jump start each time I drove the car. I needed yet another car, I needed a car that drove well, had absolutely no mechanical problems, and was great on gas. I needed a Honda.

I thought to myself I wonder if I can go to the dealership and get a used Honda. Now I had no money to put down and all I had to my name to trade in was the 1990 Cadillac that was barely drivable. I had just recently paid off my credit card debt which had previously been in collections. So I knew it was a long shot but I also felt I would be taken care of and would not be left in the cold without any transportation in a big city where the average destination is a 15-20 mile drive roundtrip. I felt a slight **peace of mind that no matter what happened at the dealership I would have reliable transportation because my spiritual parent always makes sure I am well taken care of.**

I begin to feel as if I was the son of the wealthiest being in the universe who already owns everything I need and owns everything that exists. I knew I couldn't go wrong with that kind of favor. I then felt an impression within my heart to think of the car I drove not as "MY" car but as "OUR" car, meaning that I was given the car as a gift from the universe and that the car I needed didn't belong to the dealership, the bank, or me but it truly belonged to the source of everything that exists. Therefore, I also wanted to look at the car I drove as **a gift to others as well**, meaning if

163

someone needed a ride I would be more than willing and happy to use the car I drove to help others.

I drove to the Hugh White Honda and told the salesman that greeted me that I was looking for a car that was great on gas, didn't have a lot of miles, and was no more than 10 years old. I also told him that my price range was no more than $300 a month. I filled out the application and gave him the required documents I was told to bring with me in our previous phone conversation. The salesman then left the desk to run my credit to see what vehicles I qualified for. I waited for what seemed like an eternity to discover that surprisingly my credit score was sufficient enough to qualify.

After I test drove 2 or 3 vehicles I decided upon a 2007 Honda Civic which was a newer version than I expected. All the while I was thinking that the salesman was the nicest salesman I ever encountered. I mean, he didn't pressure me or anything and made me feel very comfortable about buying a car. I felt that he had my best interest in mind. Everything was going perfect! A little too perfect.

Then……….came the big question. "How much do you want to put down on the Honda?" I was a little nervous but I managed to tell the salesman that I didn't have anything for a down payment but could trade in my barely drivable 1990 Cadillac Deville. In that very moment, in the back of my mind I thought that my qualification for the car was indeed "too good to be true." I thought to myself, "This is it!" "I won't be able to afford the monthly payment because I don't have a down payment with me."

The salesman then informed me that they appraised the Cadillac at $500 and would accept that as a down payment. He then told me the big news! He told me the news of why I had come in the first place. Yes, all the other things he told me were great! I was qualified for financing, I could get a newer model that was only three years old, and the old Cadillac that had problems starting was actually acceptable as a trade for a down payment, but what about the monthly payments?

To my surprise the salesman pushed the paperwork over to me and showed me that my monthly payment would actually be much lower than I expected to pay. I was relieved that the payment was $275 a month!

I was literally amazed that I was able to go into a dealership and drive away the same day with no money down and with mediocre credit. But I was reminded of what I had known all along, that it was a gift from the source of life that always takes care of me and that I would use it to help others as well.

Now, I said all that to say this. I could have felt that that experience was too good to be true and been suspicious that I would eventually lose the car, that somehow the dealership might call me back and say, "We overlooked a detail on your credit report and you have to bring the car back." This is what I was used to, being teased with good news or "good luck" before reality set in and I was back struggling for everything I need. However, knowing who my source is and not attributing miraculous blessings to "luck" that must have been a mistake", has kept a constant flow of provision of everything I have ever needed or even wanted.

What I mean by "knowing who my source is" is letting go of the false idea of bad luck being our fate and good luck being a mistake. It is also being open to my Higher Power reminding me that all so called luck is a gift that is purposely given by The Giver who passionately cares about me.

Appreciate Every Good Thing As A Gift

To misappropriate any good coming into our lives as a mistake or as luck makes good things temporary. However, attributing that same good to the giver of gifts that personally cares for us and then expressing a deep appreciation will ALWAYS, ALWAYS open us to receiving every good thing that we are meant to experience on frequent and constant level.

Have you ever seen the classic action movie Rocky 5? It is one of my absolute favorite childhood movies along with the entire Rocky series. One of my favorite scenes on the film is when the young protégé Tommy Gunn finally wins the fight he has been training for. Upon winning he makes a speech and says he wants to thank the man who helped him get there and thanks George Washington Duke, the man that was actually trying to take advantage of him, but fails to thank Rocky for helping him train to be a better boxer. This tragic scene of misappropriated appreciation is what I found myself doing whenever I experienced the "too good to be true". Instead of recognizing the source of my success, I mistakenly attributed the blessing or gift as random luck when I should have first acknowledged that the gift always has a giver and a purpose and then proceeded to express deep appreciation for being chosen to receive the gift.

Luck is always temporary and our enjoyment of luck leaves as soon as the luck is gone but an appreciated gift that we know the full value of is permanent, in that it fills our heart with enjoyment that cannot be lost even if we lose the gift. The permanent enjoyment that remains in spite of not having material objects is the true gift that usually comes with changing our definition from "luck" to a gift that we are chosen to receive for a specific purpose. This inner enjoyment also leaves us open to receive the "too good to be true" more frequently and longer lasting. Whichever definition we choose between luck and gifts will determine how frequent our good experiences occur and how long they last. However, it is important to remember that true luck or gifts is not the object or circumstance itself, it is solely the feeling of appreciation and savoring enjoyment that we must maintain, that is the source of ensuring we always live the "too good to be true" life.

Another experience I had that was even more surprising and specifically designed for my personal enjoyment was being able to live in my dream residence. My childhood and teen years were spent in cities no bigger than 30-40 thousand people. During high school I lived in Sandusky which is 45 minutes away from Cleveland. Although Sandusky is a tourism city known for Cedar Point, which is the largest roller coaster amusement park in the country, living in a small city made me want to visit and live in big cities. Therefore, when I moved to Columbus, Ohio the capital of my home state, I was thrilled to learn that it was the 15th largest city in the country. On top of that, I was always infatuated with downtown apartments that overlooked a skyline. Whenever I saw the high rise apartments overlooking the skyline of a big city in movies it made me want to live downtown in a big city. The only problem was apartments downtown are extremely expensive and unaffordable.

I settled and moved into an apartment that was a mile east of downtown and was really happy I could do so but I still really wanted to live directly downtown in a nice and spacious apartment. At the time I worked for the Columbus Library which has 22 branches around the city and as a job requirement I would often have to go to a training that was held at the Main branch located downtown and right next to some very attractive apartments. This piqued my interest to living downtown again so I called around and the lowest I could find was around $600 a month for a one bedroom. I didn't dare call the complex next to the library because they just looked expensive. One day I mustered up the gumption to just try to get a quote on the apartments that were next to the Main Library. I couldn't believe what I was told by the property manager. They were cheaper than what I was currently paying and there was one available to move into when my lease was up!

Both of these situations were freely given as unexpected gifts during a time that I was learning to be open to receiving ALL that Life or the Creative source behind the entire Universe had to offer me. They are but mere indications and glimpses of the full love of life that I have come to know on daily and constant basis. I believe that miraculous situations of our dreams coming true happen as we learn to recognize and appreciate each good thing that we automatically ignore. When we start to feel amazed at what we assume is just mundane everyday normalcy and recognize them as gifts specifically given to us for our personal enjoyment then we will experience miraculous amazingly good things increase in our lives.

Life Is For Us Not Against Us!

As a result of experiencing too good to be true moments where the desires of my heart happened for me, my suspicion that life was against me began to fade. The feeling that it was up to me alone to fight against the bad that was looking and lurking to attack me, turned into an excitement that looked forward to what amazing experience would happen next. It was during this time that I was made aware of one of the greatest truths that freed me from the fear that there was no real answer for the negative that plagued my life and everyone I knew. I feared that we are all hopeless against bad situation after bad situation and the only thing we have is a belief that if we pray and hope that the negative or evil goes away then we'll be protected from its imminent doom.

I am aware that this statement will offend my brothers and sisters who follow their faith but that is not my intention. My only intention is to reveal how I truly felt in my darkest times of believing and experiencing that life was out to get me because of the repetitive depressing and frustrating situations that seemed to outweigh the miraculous in my life. I truly felt that my prayers were merely a drip of water to quench the thirst of a man in hell. I wasn't sure if my prayers would work but I would try like hell to please god and be righteous so that I would be saved from the evil in this world and live a "blessed" life. The only thing was, every single time something negative or evil happened I felt worried, I felt overwhelmed, and I felt suspicious that there was no way to avoid or escape evil things taking away my ability to enjoy life.

If you are a person of faith and follow any religious teaching or worship any religious figure, maybe you have never felt that your prayers aren't enough to answer life's problems, but it was something that I felt and feared deeply. I constantly prayed for blessings and tried my very best to remain faithful. I believed that faith in god and prayer was all I needed, yet felt like the evil situations that I experienced were too much to bear and took away my ability to be free to laugh and play about life. My suspicion was that there was no real "cure" to life and that if something moderately or extremely negative happened in life that was outside of our control, there was nothing we could do to really lift the heaviness permanently and begin to fall in love with life with the giddiness and passion that we had for our first love.

This is the fear and suspicion that was starting to disappear with a new and accelerating light in my heart that was letting me know what I believed about life was a well-intentioned lie. Instead of life being against me, instead of an evil spirit or entity being behind negative situations as it seemed, I was seeing that Life was indeed rooting for me, smiling at me, and eager to unleash all good things in and through my life. This is my sole purpose in sharing my experience of transitioning from "bad luck" to accepting and living out my spiritual birth right of having every solution possible for life freely available to me and everyone. My sole purpose with the words in the book is to spread this highly contagious ease and flow in life to the precious and lovely people I share this planet with. In order to truly share this hand-crafted and designed love of life that belongs to all of us I feel that I should start with where my suspicion of good came from.

My very first introduction to the outlandish yet very real idea that life was meant and specifically designed to be thoroughly enjoyed was the lyrics to a song we sang in church when I was a young teenage Christian. This song is referred to by people of Christian faith as a "praise and worship" song but most people would call it "Church music". The title is simply called "The Happy Song" and is written by the Christian rock group called Delirious but the lyrics are as follows:

I could sing unending songs
Of how you saved my soul
I could dance a thousand miles
Because of Your great love

My heart is bursting Lord
To tell of all You've done
Of how You changed my life
And wiped away the past

Oh, I wanna shout it out
From every roof top, sing
For now I know that God
Is for me not against me

Now the lyrics speak of how the Creator makes us want to shout and burst with unending songs, and a thousand mile dances but the most telling portion of these lyrics is it is all because we now know that "God is for me not against me".

I Soooooo wanted to feel this way, but truly and honestly, no matter how many times I sang this song with fervor, I did not feel this in my religious pursuit of a connection with the Source of all existence. My outlook on faith at the time was one of having to "find" God, who was obviously hiding from his creation and family of human beings. At the time I believed and envisioned this hidden mystery man as a white, translucent male that gave me goose bumps in church services. I firmly believed that "he" would be so kind as to not throw me over to Satan's power into Hell because I pleased "him" and did what "he" required of me through the Bible and the Christian church leaders who explained what God wanted from me in order for me to find him. I fervently practiced this lifestyle of being obsessed with pleasing the religious version of the Source of existence with my religious deeds for approximately nine years.

The only problem I ran into with my hot pursuit of the Creator was the burning questions of; if I was chasing god, then was god running away from me? Does god want to be found? Was god hiding from the people he wanted to find him? Was this experience of dancing and singing about life only available for Christians? Was it for the Muslim? Was it for the homosexual? Was it for the drug addict? Was it for the homeless person? Was it for the most unloved and undesirable of the human race? Was it truly for me? What a paradox! I began asking for explanations to these provocative and controversial questions but no longer to the Christian leaders whom I still adore very deeply.

It had become such an obsession of mine to find god that I began praying constantly, directly asking my honest inquiries to the higher power itself? "Are you hiding from me, yet desire me to find you? If so, why?" It became my quest to have this experience of dancing for a thousand miles and singing unending songs because of how happy, excited, and ultimately ecstatic I was about life and my existence. If only I could know that god was for me, not against me.

The lyrics to this song sent me on a Alice in Wonderland style adventure to have this experience yet was desperately perplexed because all I had heard or thought I heard from my well intentioned Christian parents, Sunday school teachers, and church leaders was that god was indeed against me. How could I have possibly been taught that the very definition of the purest form of love could be against me? Now, I didn't literally hear the sentence, "God doesn't love you and is personally routing for your failure and destruction." I indirectly learned this suspicion of my Creator's life giving love for me by being taught that I was "born a sinner", meaning that when I was born I was automatically doomed to be offensive to the creator and my very existence as a human being was offensive to god because it was my natural desire to commit deeds that displeased him to the point of eventual destruction. It was this impending doom that dictated my mandatory need to be saved from this destruction. It was this protection from destruction from endless burning that was "the good news" that was supposed to set my feet to dancing for thousands of miles and my mouth to sing endless songs of joy. So how can I find this god's love, whose extreme displeasure with who I was and what I did would cause me to be forever alienated from him and tortured, beyond what I could possibly imagine or witness in the scariest horror movie?

I truly accepted that I had to beg for forgiveness for the offensive way I was born without my consent. I truly accepted his only way of living my life and obeying his commands in order to escape his wrath. This seemingly never ending contradiction of me knowing that god was so easily upset with me and also at the same instant causing me to dance and sing endlessly caused me to want this experience even more; **even if I had to experience it without what I believed about god**.

It was from this paradox of feeling loved by an angry invisible and invincible entity that created my suspicion of enjoying an amazingly good life being possible for me. What if what I had been told about the Creator was a misconception? What if I didn't have to be introduced to the Source of my life from a third party? And the even more dangerous question was, what if the well-meaning dear people who truly loved me were mistaken about an age old story about god which didn't come with love without conditions that I am supposed to experience and produce as a result.

I want to take a moment to repeat that my intention is not to offend or upset any people of faith who believe and practice the experience that I just mentioned. I only wish to share my experience in that when I was really honest and open with myself, my belief in these teachings about god's wrath and judgment caused me to not truly enjoy my life with god as a Christian or even enjoy my life as a human being for that matter. This is where my personal suspicion of good being possible originated.

If you happen to be a Christian who has chosen to read this book and believe these things and honestly enjoy and love your relationship with the Creator then who am I to know your heart and say that you don't. All I can say is that I didn't and personally know several people who did not experience the unconditional love, joy, peace, and righteousness that is supposed to be the natural result of following Christ through believing in the bible. Also, I cannot share my experience of living a truly blessed and life full of joy and wonder without retelling this experience the way that I felt it happened for me.

Now, as I began to honestly pray from my heart and ask for the bottom line to what this life is all about and why I wasn't experiencing the abundant life promised to me as a believer in Christ, I begin to feel more and more that it was because of my misappropriated trust in man's feeble attempt at explaining god. I began to feel more and more that is was because I was not aware of my connection with the true spirit that is the source of all life that causes me to know peace and joy in life was possible for me personally. I was discovering, that everything I had learned about god did not come from the Creator itself but from what human beings told me.

I began to imagine if god was a real person if those character traits would be someone I would want a relationship with. What if I had a relationship with someone who told me that there was something inherently wrong with me and that I needed to live only the way they told me to live if I had any hope of being happy? What if someone that told me if I did not accept and completely follow their control of my life that I would be cursed and doomed to torture and suffering? What is someone would literally allow horrible things to happen to me without remedy, that they had the power to prevent but didn't because of my failure to obey them. What if I knew someone that everything I learned about them came from a third party and did not allow me to see, hear and get to meet and know them personally for myself. Imagine that if you will.

Someone wants to meet you but hides from you and only communicates to you through another person who supposedly knows them better than you do but is retelling all this persons characteristics that include demand for complete and total obedience or else be cursed to complete and total misery and eventually destruction.

More and more I saw and felt that this idea might be false and was only told to me by well-meaning people who it had been told to as well. I knew the people that told me these things loved me but were also victims of this myth about the source of life that was several generations old. Somebody or somebodies had perpetuated what can only be called a lie and caused descendants of a spiritual royalty known as the human race to believe that they were mere peasants and dogs begging for the scraps at the royal table of the universe but didn't know they are the sons and daughters of the ruler of the kingdom.

What I am speaking of is experiencing god without religion, without teachings you have to believe, and rituals you have to practice in order to please a distant entity and be protected from his wrath. As a Christian, whenever I told my friends and family about Jesus and they said, "I'm not religious", I would respond by saying "I'm not talking about religion, I'm talking about a relationship." This is why I asked earlier in this chapter to imagine as if I wanted to introduce you to a person who I told you behaved as we are told god behaves towards us and requires what we are told god requires of us. It is now my belief that we are natural inheritors and it is our birth right as human beings sent to earth with the sole mission to truly experience good in life and an ecstatic love of life.

This is what the "too good to be true" life is! It is dancing and singing about how overwhelming good life has been to us. We can now know that we do not have to pray, beg, and plead an intangible being for good to happen *to* us, but that we inherently possess the goodness that flows from *within* us.

I did not come to know and experience this until I was willing to let go of the cause of my suspicion which was that my Creator was not pleased with me and I needed spend my life desperately earning his favor to avoid his wrath. Once I was willing to let go of this suspicion I could see that goodness was indeed meant and specifically designed for me instead of just a random entity that was somewhere out there and if I follow a religious tradition, can briefly experience its goodness. All I want to do is let us all know that this goodness in life is specifically meant for all of us and that it is not merely for us to briefly taste after we do the right things. However, I have now come to sense the overwhelming goodness of feeling elated and bursting about life that can be **lived** as often as we breathe and not just randomly experienced.

The first process for me in living this song and dance about life was letting go of my superstitious myth about life, that it was reluctantly and hesitantly good. For me that superstitious belief of not fully trusting that I was meant to experience good things as a birth right came from falsely seeking to find god through religion presented as a loving relationship with an invisible being. My sincere mistake was simply believing every word that I was told about something I could literally encounter and know for myself, which is the source of energy that makes me alive, not a religious mythical figure.

You see my religious leaders loved me and I love them but that doesn't mean that it is impossible for me to be misled by what they taught me; just like when our parents let us believe in Santa Claus or the Tooth Fairy. Our parents love us but they do mislead us into believing in myths that bring us good if we are good boys and girls. Misleading doesn't always mean it is predatory. So I don't think of myself as a victim of deception. I just believe that what I was told about god and the meaning of life was the age old telephone game where something true is told to one person, it gets whispered to the next person's ear until by the time it gets to me it is a completely different statement. To avoid this, we must hear the message straight from the horse's mouth for ourselves.

The "too good to be true" life did not happen for me until I was free to hear it directly from the horse's mouth indeed. The horse of course being, the source that thought me up and placed me on this planet among billions of galaxies. What was the true reason for this assignment on earth? This question directed to the originator of the mission was the beginning of the "too good to be true". I was beginning to see that god was not a pimp that told me I would never be happy without complete allegiance to him. I was beginning to see that that god was not a terrorist with demands in exchange for escaping torture. I was beginning to see that god is not what the church says about it and that god is only what it says about itself;

the spirit of all that exists and especially the spirit of my life personally. We can all experience for ourselves an awareness of the connection we have with the source.

Through my awareness of this connection I came to realize that this source is purely *spirit* so that it cannot have any human characteristics such as gender, race, or feeble human emotions like revenge and jealousy. Therefore, from my experience this source is love itself without any condition. When we really encounter and receive this love it makes us want to float in mid-air and jump and leap about with immense pleasure about our existence simply because we are who we are and not because of what we did or didn't do. This is the answer I received to my nagging question of why god was hiding if I am supposed to find "him". This was the answer that released the "too good to be true" into my life as a constant expression as opposed to a periodic experience.

So now I would like to ask you, as the reader, the bold questions that I asked myself:

How do you respond when anything positive or good happens in your life?

Do you, like me, subconsciously believe that it is only temporary and hope that the good experience lasts?

Do you subconsciously fear or mistrust that the bad experiences you are used to will eventually repeat themselves after the good experience passes?

Are you suspicious that goodness in life and positive experiences are not genuinely meant for you and are just random teases? And most importantly, what, if anything, do you believe is the cause of that suspicion?

Perhaps, it is a life full of traumatizing negative experiences that cause us to naturally attempt to protect ourselves from being hurt or disappointed again and so we dare not hope or get excited about anything good being a constant mainstay in our lives. It is like when a child has been physically abused and if a caring adult reaches to hug them, they duck just from the mere sensitivity of it reminding the child of being hit and causing them to instinctively protect themselves from being hurt again. We can duck a good and loving touch because it is heading towards the same area that has been hurt one too many times. That is how it is when we experience something good in our lives or if there is a great potential for a positive experience if we were to cooperate with an act to receive it but it makes us uncomfortable. We are leery of whether it is worth it to inconvenience ourselves and trust that a change of heart, a change in perspective, and ultimately a change in lifestyle will result in a greater return on our investment, so to speak. Is what we are giving up in emotional and mental comfort and convenience less than what we will be an added benefit as a result? We want to give a minimal amount of inner willingness to cooperate with anything other than our emotional safe haven of how we have always coped with a negative experience. So let me re-ask us a consequential question that I asked earlier in the book.

How do you emotionally and mentally respond when you experience something negative?

Just for a moment, ignore any mental distractions. It may even help to close your eyes and mentally recall what you think about when you are in the midst of an experience that is frustrating or depressing on any level.

How did you feel during the most recent negative experience you had?

Why do you typically respond the same way when someone offends or challenges you?

Why do you typically respond the same way if something negative happens that you feel you didn't deserve but nonetheless it's an experience that makes you feel frustrated, depressed, distraught, or confused?

Initially you may draw a blank or be uncomfortable answering these questions but if we ask them out loud to ourselves or even voice them within ourselves waiting silently for our minds to give us answer will make it an easier process.

I am also taking a brief break from writing this to ask my all-knowing higher self the same questions.

Doing this self-reflective exercise can be surprisingly freeing because **the subconscious is behind the majority, if not all of our repeating negative experiences.** As a result, **this process of being aware and breaking our subconscious negative responses is the beginning to being able to free ourselves from the prison of subconsciously expecting and accepting the repetition of negative experiences to be the story of our lives.** Therefore, ending the cycle of merely hoping, wishing, and praying that our lives will get better and feeling suspicious and leery of the "too good to be true" life where we are pleasantly surprised, wowed, and being swept off of our feet by life on a daily basis.

So, picking up where we left off in asking ourselves out loud, "How do I feel during my negative experiences and why do I typically respond that way?" I asked myself this as well and waited in silence for my heart to give me an answer for my own spiritual growth. What I heard for myself is that I take too much pride in being intelligent and feel as if I am more intelligent than others who offend me and become very defensive of any criticism directed towards me because it makes me feel inferior, unintelligent, and like I don't know what I'm doing.

I also became aware of the fact that if someone challenges me and makes an aggressive gesture towards me that I respond with extreme anger to assure that they do not attempt to take advantage of me ever again and to prove that, "I am not to be f__ed with!"

Lastly, if I personally experience bad or devastating news, where I find myself in negative circumstances or series of life events, I typically over think how to never experience that circumstance again and become stressed to figure out an intelligent way to escape the situation and avoid it all together the next time around.

So, now comes the tricky part of the question when I asked "why do I typically respond that way?" to discover the subconscious cause of my suspicion of good.

I asked this of myself out loud and I heard my heart tell me that I don't like getting "in trouble" so to completely avoid feeling like a screw up, like I have felt for most of my life, I strive to outsmart anyone and anything. Also, as I shared earlier, I fear rejection. I don't like when anyone doesn't like me or criticizes me, or tries to be aggressive with me. I am constantly trying to prove myself so that my family, friends, co-workers, the children and teens I work with, and everyone I meet likes and approves of me. If anyone shows in any way that they don't like me, then that is the worst thing in the entire world to me because I have a deathly fear of rejection. I didn't feel accepted by my peers and family members because I was a sensitive momma's boy and not tough enough to defend myself. So now as an adult I am able to defend myself with being intelligent and responsible and take too much pride in my intelligence and responsibility because I want to make sure I cannot be criticized for any reason and that I am accepted because of it. Now there is nothing wrong with being intelligent and reliable but when I am doing it to find approval and acceptance and to keep people from criticizing or rejecting me then it can be spiritually unhealthy.

I became aware of these heavy revelations about my subconscious self in the moment it took me to ask that two part question and believe that my heart would provide the answer. This process is something I had to do before I was even able to open myself up to be in a position to expect and accept the "too good" that the universe is eager to lavishly provide to me. Once I learned to expect and accept the "too good to be true", unbelievable goodness replaced my expecting and accepting of negative circumstances.

This process was key in getting to the place in my spiritual journey to be able to acknowledge and appreciate all the good that I ignore and overlook on a constant basis. **I had to realize that I am mentally conditioned to be blind to my daily miracles that are constantly being given to me and instead live in mental complaining about my many inconveniences.** This self-assessment process mainly gives me the ability to really believe that god, the ultimate good, love, and the source of life is really truly for me and has no greater desire than to spoil me with blessings and miracles and wants to do good for me more than I want good from it.

This force of pure love has my very best interest in mind and I don't have to be suspicious that something bad outside of my control will befall me and overtake me. I don't have to be concerned about a stingy source that withholds the good things that I need to fully enjoy life. I can now clearly sense that my source is overwhelmingly abundant by nature and is constantly lavishly filling my life with all I need to fully enjoy my existence.

I have come to find that this is the biggest and most important myth and misconception about god and why we all exist, that religion has unintentionally lied to us about. The age old myth that we are here to serve god as minions and servants instead of enjoying the feeling of a strong connection in life that levitates us to a state of sheer hysteria about our existence and oneness with our creator and source. The closest feeling to it in human form is how we feel about our children in their most innocent, creative, imaginative, and cutest moments. Our perception of where we originate from must progress from one of a stoic judge to a generous elated parent.

Now we can know that religion does not equal god as we have mistakenly believed. Religion is the story about god told by flawed humans passed down generation after generation. Having to perform any practice to avoid the threat of being punished is religion in its truest form. But now we can feel and enjoy our connection with our source of existence without the threat of being a disappointment to our spiritual parent, without the threat of asking for something we need to enjoy life and being told we are not good enough to deserve it. So now we are no longer mere servants that perform a job description as housekeepers of the earth. We know and feel like the earth and the entire universe is ours as much as it is our Creators. We know and feel that the possibilities are literally endless and unrestricted. We know and feel that anything that we could ever possibly need or want to more fully enjoy life, that our source more so wants it for us than we want it for ourselves and all that is needed to receive this endless and constant influx of goodness and enjoyment is simply trust.

We can trust that the source of the entire universe is for us not against us. We can trust that even though life has disappointed us and hurt us, that doesn't mean that is the "story of our lives" or our fate is to repeat that. We can trust that we can specifically ask for anything we need big or small, impossible or attainable with confidence. Even if we don't exactly know what we want or need in life, we can trust our source to take care of and cover everything so that we find that we are regularly surprised by goodness that we didn't even ask for.

So now I ask you as the reader and co-traveler on this spiritual journey to loving our lives to the fullest degree; are you suspicious that your life can be truly too good to be true, if so, what is the source of your suspicion? What did you hear from your heart when you asked about how you respond in negative situations and why you typically respond that way?

Now can we all do one last step together to truly unleash the too good into our lives? Take what you realized about how you cope with the negative and simply **be willing to give it up**. Be willing to no longer rely on our own self-preservation and self-protection from being offended, disappointed, and hurt and be open to trusting that you are taken care of by the same force that made you and wanted you to exist as a human being. That same force is now all you need to enjoy life. It is not your sole responsibility to look out for and take care of yourself. If you so desire, you can be treated far better than you treat yourself by a loving force that will pour upon us all we need to fully love every single thing about our existence. This happens as we allow it to truly be our source, not just of our physical existence, but more so the source of our daily experiences.

Dancing And Singing About Life!

So now, you and I can voice what it is we feel we need to enjoy life right now and ask our spiritual parent to freely give it to us. Whatever wisdom and understanding is needed to steward and manage the gift of life then we can accept and receive that as well. The idea is to experience life as "too good to be true" but when we are pleasantly surprised by goodness in our lives know that every good thing is truly specifically thought up by our source and given to us with pleasure, just to see us smile and show us how special we are. So let us smile and take pleasure in our lives as we dance with the source that gives us life. Let us embrace and receive every single good thing that our spiritual parent is freely offering to us.

Now finally, there is a difference between being spoiled to be selfish and have material outward success and being spoiled with goodness to have an inner wealth of immense pleasure and enjoyment with our lives and existence. I can't reiterate enough that this inner excitement about our life is the true easy and good life. However, I will reference two stories from an ancient text to clearly illustrate what living "too good to be true" looks like in real life.

As I mentioned earlier, living and experiencing life being too good to be true yet knowing with confidence that this level of uninhibited free goodness is indeed true is when we feel like dancing for a thousand miles and singing a thousand songs from the rooftops. So how do get from begging for Life to bless us and help us with our problems to feeling like dancing and singing about our lives.

Let's pay attention to an old story of a man crippled from birth who was begging for money outside of a church service. Two minsters walking into the church stop to look intently at the crippled man begging for money, and say to him, "We do not have any money but what we do have, we pass along to you." One of the ministers then grabbed the crippled man's hand and pulled him to his feet and commanded the man to walk. The man then leaped forward and began to walk and then leap. He kept jumping and leaping with excitement into the church all while feeling and saying how full of appreciation he was to the Creator. (Acts 3:1-10)

Wow! What a story. If we are going to feel this way about our lives we can notice a few key things that happen in the story. First the man was crippled, meaning he could not walk the walk so to speak. An even better way to say it is he could not move forward in life. Whenever he attempted to physically move forward he would stumble and crash back to the ground. I experienced this crippling inability to move forward in life and crashing with every attempt for a long, long time!

Next he was begging for money. Desiring material success is our natural instinct whenever we as humans cannot seem to do good for ourselves even when we try our hardest. We try and try for so long only to keep crashing so our only option left is to stop trying and beg for somebody, anybody to help us attain material success. Ultimately, we are looking for the same thing the crippled man was looking for out of life. He didn't ask for help with his true problem of not being able to walk. He asked for something that would make him feel better about not being able to walk. He asked for money so that maybe just maybe he could buy some alcohol or food to eat to take his mind off the pain of not being able to physically move forward on his own. We do the same thing every day whenever we can't move forward in life on our own, we look for material success. We really want a nice house, a luxury car, an attractive supportive mate, and adoring children…all symbols of outward success. But we only desire what is actually a distraction from what we really need. We don't mention or seek the antidote to not being able to move forward with life, we desire and seek after living an outwardly good life of material wealth. This is precisely why the minister told the man he didn't have any material success to give to him but he could give him something even better than wealth. Even better than wealth? Yes, far better! Like, not even close, better!

He gives him the ability to feel ecstatic about life. You see the greatest miracle in the story was not that the crippled man could now walk. It was that the crippled man, after years of hanging his head low, and feeling absolutely hopeless and helpless, could smile again, and go around leaping and jumping for joy because of how he felt on the inside.

So what the minister was really saying was two key things that we can learn to look for out of life. "I don't have any money" is really saying that a "better life" is not what you really need. What you really need is better than a good life full of material success. What you really need is pure and uninhibited joy!

The other key that we can learn from this telling story is that the crippled man wanted some money to temporarily help his outside circumstances but what he got was the ability the feel like he was rich on the inside, forever. Just based on how he was expressing his sheer enjoyment I would say it was safe to say that he felt like a million bucks which far exceeds having a million bucks but feeling like a poor crippled man. There is a very vast difference between living what many consider the good life on the outside and living the good life on the inside by having the feeling of having the entire universe at your very fingertips.

You see, you can have several individual luxurious items that you can attain from material success and wealth which by the way can all be lost, stolen, or spent with bad circumstances OR you can have the power to get wealth where everything you touch turns to gold, where you live a truly amazingly miraculous life, where the impossible, the unthinkable, the unbelievable lives easily and freely in and through you. One is lived and experienced solely on the outside through circumstances. The other is lived and experienced solely on the inside through enjoying life. One is based on attaining material circumstances that only appear to improve life. The other is based on feeling amazing especially when horrible things happen. The difference between the two can be better explained by a story about a man who lost his son.

There was a very wealthy man who had two sons and the younger son asked his father for his inheritance. The father divided his estate between the sons and a few days later the younger son took his inheritance and traveled to a faraway country and wasted all of his inheritance by spending money without any restraint. After he spent all he had there was a famine in that country so it was impossible to find food. He then begged a citizen of the country for work, who put him to work feeding hogs. While he was working and feeding the hogs he was so hungry that he considered eating what the hogs were eating. Then he came to his senses and said to himself, "How many of my father's servants have enough food to throw away but here I am literally dying of hunger. I will go to my father, admit I was wrong for wasting my inheritance and tell him I am no longer worthy to be called your son, just make one of your hired servants."

So he got up and started to walk home, but while he was still a long way off, his father saw him and was moved with compassion and tenderness towards him and he ran and embraced and kissed his son passionately. Then the father said to his servants, go get the special robe of honor, a ring for his finger, and sandals for his feet. Prepare the fattest cow for a feast and let us make noise as we enjoy ourselves with dancing and drinking and make everyone feel alive with cheer!" (Luke 15:11-32)

Imagine the feeling the young rebellious son must have felt in his heart. Imagine how relieved and joyous he must have felt when he saw his father waiting and looking for him after all that time. You see, the son thought that the father surely was upset with him and would never fully forgive his rebellion and disobedience. He thought that he would have to hang his head low and feel miserable as he approached his father. What he actually experienced was full delight and pleasure that he was home and was exuberantly celebrated with royal living and lively cheering! This is how life is truly meant to be!

What we assume life is, is a misery and shame that causes us to feel as servants to the Creator, when all the while our Creator takes sheer delight in us and sees us only as equals. Everything the Creator is we are and everything the Creator has we have. We only need to know this and that desiring and seeking a better life and material success in life is like eating and wallowing around with pigs when we are really the sons and daughter of a King, just like Mephibosheth who is mentioned earlier in the book. We need not falsely believe that the good life is what we accomplish, possess, and what people think about us. The amazingly good life is this feeling of an all-out celebration that the Creator is so passionate and delighted with us that it wants us to feel about ourselves the same way it feels about us: Thrilled and Overjoyed!

The real problem the son had was not that he disobeyed and lost everything and was reduced to groveling to his father for messing everything up. That is the way I have always heard this biblical parable interpreted by church leaders: that the lost son had to apologize with remorse in order to gain his father's good graces back. However, that is not what the story tells me. It tells me that the father was looking for him and saw him while he was a long way off; that means the father wasn't concerned about the disobedience the son committed. The father was only concerned with his son's well-being and every day, for several hours a day, went out to look for his son passionately desiring for him to return. Therefore, **the son's real problem was that he didn't know how his father really felt about him** when he left with his inheritance. He thought that possessions, accomplishments, and approval from others were all he needed to enjoy life, when really the love of his father was far better than the inheritance of riches.

So what can we do to easily activate this level of celebration of our lives? We need not come to the Creator as humble servants who work for leftovers or second best as the lost son assumed he would have to be demoted. We only need to communicate with the Creator as pure, innocent, imaginative, and energetic children.

Releasing Our Inner-Child

When we do this we will experience the true and undeniable greatest life we ever imagined and it will include these three defining experiences:

1. Feeling an immeasurable amount of pleasure with ourselves. It is simply eternally smiling at ourselves in everything and at all times. It is knowing everything we are and everything about us is RIGHT. It is knowing that we can literally do no wrong because all wrong is made right when we forgive ourselves when we do things that cause negativity to persist in our own lives and cause negativity in the lives of others, just like the lost son experienced. This is what ancient spiritual texts describe as righteousness.

2. Feeling like everything we touch turns to gold, feeling like the luckiest, most blessed being in all the universe and that literally nothing can go wrong for us because even when something appears negative it's purpose is to only add to our inner riches and wealth in life and is a part of literally every single thing that happens in our lives, good or bad, positive or negative, working out to our benefit and favor. This is what ancient spiritual texts describe as peace.

3. Feeling like every day is our birthday and celebrating and having a wild party for ourselves. It is simply feeling like a kid at Christmas, feeling like all the magic, mystery, and goodness we believed in as children is real to the point that we can't stop laughing and playing with every ounce of our energy. While it is not believing in Santa Claus, it is indeed the part of us that made us believe that a Santa was possible, flourishing without anything or anyone dousing out our passionate fire for life. This

is what ancient spiritual texts describe as joy.

Then how is this level of true righteousness, peace, and joy experienced and expressed in human life? There is a story about the enlightened teacher Jesus that tells us how to simply yet certainly live this life:

In the story Jesus' followers asked him who can have the highest level of righteousness, peace, and joy (pleasure, favor, and uninhibited playful joy) in their life. Jesus responded by calling a child to come to him and said to his followers, **"The key is to change how you think about life now as an adult and think like a small child.** If you cannot do this, you cannot experience pleasure, favor, and joy. If you inspire anyone to think and feel like a small child (playful and trusting of good) you will welcome and accept the presence of these 3 key experiences in your life. If you cause anyone to no longer trust that the universe is good, no longer play and laugh with the fullness of energy, and no longer imagine the impossible is real then you will not have the privilege of living with these 3 key experiences." (Matthew 18:1-6)

In another similar story people were bringing children to Jesus for him to say a blessing for the children but his followers tried to stop so many children from bothering Jesus. Then Jesus said to his followers, "allow all the children to come to me without hesitation because pleasure, favor, and playful uninhibited joy belong to people who are like these children." Again, if we approach life as innocent and energetic children, and inspire and allow others to do the same then we will always have pleasure, favor, and laugh and play with energy. (Matthew 19:13-15)

What is it about a child that is so special; that it unlocks the secret to living life how is designed to be lived? From what I observe in my job at the library working with children on their homework during the school year and serving them free lunch during the summer, there are several key characteristics that children naturally possess. Teenagers, adults, and the elderly still have these within them and can release them at any time but children automatically and constantly express them with no effort.

- First and foremost children are trusting. If an adult tells them most any ridiculous absurd fact, children will believe it is true for at least a moment if not for lifetime.

- Children are inquisitive and curious, always asking, looking, observing while their little brains swirl with questions about why adults and the world around them operate the way they do. They are on a constant mission to discover whatever they do not know yet.

- Children are imaginative and always thinking of new ways for them to do what they do best; play and have fun. If you leave a child with no toys or television for very long, watch and see how they make believe and pretend all kinds of games and playmates for themselves.

- Children have limitless potential. If you spend enough time with any child you will notice important qualities about them now that will grow and flourish into a very special skill as they grow into adolescence and adult hood. Children that can paint the most abstract pictures as they play may one day grow to design the most fabulous fashion designs for the clothes we wear. Children that know how to take things apart and put them back together will design the newest technology we'll all be using in the next 20 years. For it was the child who always got bad grades in school and came home and boiled several cans of tomato sauce just to see them explode all over the kitchen walls and floor that became the great visual movie director Stephen Spielberg!

So the key question we can ask ourselves is, do we feel and think like adults who anticipate harm and protect ourselves from being disappointed even from anything that is actually good and what we need? Or do we feel and think about life like small children who are trusting of good, eager to be aware of the fullness of what life has to offer, imagining that the impossible is all too real, and expressing our limitless potential to design and innovate new creations?

If not, then let us ask our spiritual parent, the source of all life the most important prayer or meditation we can ever ask or desire. "Let me feel and think like a small child, let all of the amazement, gullibility, imagination, and playful energy that you have given all of us, spill out of me like a never ending fountain. May it no longer be hidden, stifled, and detained with fear by the seemingly dark and negative in the world, but let it flow freely with complete abandon like a lively breeze in the spring that blows over me. Let it glow like a warm tingling light that guides and shines through me so that all of life becomes magically and mysteriously easy!"

The good news is that we can never express too many child-like qualities of the love of life. Even when we all too often feel everything but child-like, when we feel depressed, distraught, frustrated, disappointed, unenthusiastic, skeptical, and suspicious about life as an adult whose natural instincts are mistrust, we can still know that we no longer have to mistrust the possibility of amazingly good things happening for us and we do not have to stop being playful about life as adults. We can still know that the benefit of being an adult is to now have the insight and wisdom to discern what good we can trust and open ourselves up to and what is a deception and not meant for us to experience.

The good news is also that we can always simply give the essential but hidden qualities of children, that we eternally possess, permission to flow forth out of our inner most being into every area of our lives. This will unlock a rush of energy that allows us to feel and know with everything that we are, that every single solitary good thing that happens in our lives is a specific gift hand-picked and specifically given to us for our very own personal enjoyment.

The even better news is that when we can give ourselves this permission to trust that life is amazingly good to us and believe in the impossible, we will find ourselves always immeasurably pleased with our lives, highly favored, and overly thrilled at how easy and good life is.

Afterword
Part 1
For Christians using the Bible
As a spiritual guide

Life More Abundantly

Being frustrated with our personal relationship with god is all too common for people of faith. I have had many conversations with followers of Christ about their faith that was similar to what caused me to seek more out of my experience with god. Every believer or person of faith has had their fair share of frustrations, questions, concerns, and burdens that seem to never ever be alleviated. Although there are several individual instances that we feel god's presence and are comforted and inspired, we still wrestle with that burning grievance of not living our lives of faith full of liberty to enjoy life.

To put it in terms believers can understand: **We feel as if we are not living life more abundantly, we do not feel like more than conquerors in Christ, we do not feel like we are one with Christ as he is one with god, we do not feel the peace that passes all**

understanding, and we do not feel unspeakable joy.
In fact, we feel distanced from god and are fighting hard to remain faithful so that we do not stumble and we subconsciously fear god's wrath and punishment if we allow our faith to slip. Believe me when I tell you that I have, all too well, been there and done that!

These specific frustrations, questions, concerns, and burden's that we carry with us so heavily are very valid. Yet, they are also of extreme importance to explore and follow their instincts in order to feel and experience the daily freedom and liberty to fully enjoy life with our creator.

All too often we have subconsciously or directly asked ourselves that daunting question: Am I truly enjoying my life as a Christian? If we are truly honest and real about how we feel about our connection to the creator we will get a definite answer but we also fear what that answer may be. However, if the honest answer we give ourselves is indeed that we feel frustrated, confused, empty, and alone then I believe exploring these raw and honest feelings are the beginning to enjoying a very deep and real connection with the creator that causes us to be amazed at how awesome life is.

The only problem to this solution is that we may have silenced that question with pre-programmed answers that we have been taught to tell ourselves so that we don't lose faith. We may be afraid to ask very real and honest questions directly to our creator and fear that we lack faith. With that fear of losing faith we may dismiss our true feelings and tell ourselves, "In this life you will have many trials", or "he who endures til the end will be saved", or even the all too popular "We know not the mind of god....His ways are not our ways".

These affirmations are meant to encourage us to fight through the genuine frustrations, questions, and burdens we carry. However, what we may fail to realize, whenever we have a pre-designed answer to dismiss heartfelt concerns, is that we are not being honest with our creator. And so we "fight the good fight of faith" by dismissing genuine doubts and fears with memorized verses from scripture as opposed to being able to honestly express our heart to our source without the filter that has been taught to us by our beloved well-meaning Christian parents, Sunday school teachers, and church leaders.

Being open with the creator about my frustrations with life and having a willingness to change what I believed about god opened me up to living life more abundantly as promised in John 10:10. The most important question we must ask ourselves is,

"If Jesus says his sole purpose is for me to live life to the fullest or more abundantly, then am I truly enjoying life to the fullest?"

If not, then we must further evaluate through spiritual soul searching why we aren't enjoying life to the fullest. What I found was that my sincere yet misguided beliefs about my faith in Christ were so entrenched that I was unwilling to let them go and believe the spiritual truths that would surely set me free to fully enjoy life because they were in total opposition to what Christianity taught me.

If we feel like our faith is not working for us or if we are not truly experiencing the blessings we believe are given to believers we should be brutally honest about our disillusionment in our communication with the creator. We can also ask for a willingness to follow our true spiritual path led by our inner spirit instead of man-made guidance.

Blind Leading The Blind

These feelings of frustrations, questions, concerns, and burdens were the beginning of my true journey with the Spirit who led me to a true and genuine peace that is so surprising that it cannot be understood and an enjoyment so overwhelming that it can't even be put into words. I knew it was possible, but when I didn't experience it through the spiritual disciplines of attending church, memorizing and quoting scripture, prayer, and fasting, I felt as if Jesus may have saved my soul from hell but what good was it if he did not save my soul from living hell on earth.

I desperately wanted the two to correspond with each other. A salvation from eternal punishment was no good to me unless I experienced a salvation into a peace of mind and enjoyment of life prior to the afterlife. This peace of mind did not even begin to appear until I no longer looked to my Christian leaders for my primary counsel and directed all of my feelings of frustration directly to my spiritual parent as my sole source of clarity. I was learning that although it is good to find wisdom in the company of many counselors (Proverbs 15:22); it is just as well foolish to follow the doctrines that men teach us not to question. It is like a blind man guiding another blind man (Matthew 15:1-14).

You see I felt as though I was indeed blind and confused on where to go to find the fullness of love that I needed. I was following the biblical teaching and advice from well-meaning yet flawed humans whom I dearly love and appreciate. However, there came a point of desperation after I had so many meetings with pastors, Christian counselors, apostles, and prophets and did not experience the wisdom I needed to simply enjoy life. Yes I was going to heaven; yes I would make the rapture…Great! But how do I just like myself? How do I just enjoy my life? I believed their counsel and words of divine revelation would lead me to heaven but what was I going to do about today while I was still on earth.

I mistakenly assumed the only two options were to either completely give up on my faith through abandoning those spiritual disciplines I had been taught were my only connection with god or continue telling myself those scriptural answers to life's problems, while in the process ignoring what truly connects us to our source. I believe that what truly connects us to our source is honestly expressing what we think and feel directly to our spiritual parent without any learned religious tone or wording.

So I just continued to tell myself those scriptural answers to my very real and deep concerns and burdens I had carried so heavily since childhood. All the while not knowing how to express how I really felt to our source and at the same time sound holy, submissive, reverent, and obedient. However, what I came to realize is that I could no longer do both. I could no longer do the juggling act of approaching our source as I was "supposed to" AND have a real connection with it. I had to choose one or the other. Did I want to keep up appearances of my faith so I could make the rapture or did I want to enjoy life today? I began to have the itching suspicion within the depths of my heart that if I wanted a true and real connection with source and if I wanted the intimate relationship of walking with source as Jesus walked with God, then I could not do what I was "supposed to do" any longer. I had to come real or not at all.

The frustrations, questions, concerns, and burdens I experienced when I was going through this process started with feeling dry or not feeling god's presence for long periods of time. This feeling evolved into a desire to experience heaven here on earth as we pray in the Lord's Prayer. Waiting until I died to walk streets of gold was not as appealing if I could not enjoy life today.

Heaven on earth meant peace whenever there was the potential to worry about a bad situation, still enjoying life whenever there was the potential to get depressed or angry about life, and still feeling a love and even a like for myself whenever there was the potential to feel ashamed of myself.

So I made a risky decision and began to just simply address the creator through very honest prayers. I completely let my religious guard down and just came to god as Jason. I no longer started off with "Heavenly Father". I no longer sounded programmed, submissive, and reserved. I was desperate and so I sounded as such. I cursed in my prayers. I yelled at times. I cried at times. I demanded at times.

How irreverent and blasphemous right? But the more I asked to really know god for myself the more I felt like I should be as brutally honest as possible. I felt like god was telling me that he was a "big boy" and could handle me being real and honest with him.

A Servant Or A Son?

At the height of my most sincere heartfelt inquiries to god about how to enjoy life, I heard a freeing response within my heart. What I heard was not what I expected to hear from god but set me on an entirely new spiritual journey where I felt a much closer connection with the creator. What I heard was a series of questions that changed my perception of who the creator is and how it feels about me.

The questions I sensed in my heart were: "Who told you that you had to perform spiritual disciplines to have a connection with me?

Who told you that you had to quote scripture in response to your genuine concerns?

What if I were a real parent and I told you that you had to memorize a letter I wrote to you and that in order to talk to me you would have to only speak in those terms and that if you ever swayed from the instructions in the letter not only would I leave you to be persecuted but I would allow my worst enemy to take you into never ending torture to be burned forever?

If your earthly parents would not do that then why would I?"

I was scared! This went against every single thing I had heard and learned to believe was absolute truth with no room for questioning. The consequences for this kind of insubordination and individuality was excommunication from my community of faith, an eternal sentence of being left behind to be tortured when Jesus returned for the faithful, and soon thereafter thrown into a never ending blazing fire to be destroyed. I DID NOT want this to be my fate so I battled and wrestled with whether or not releasing my real concerns to god and exposing my true and unholy self was actually from god's guidance. I kept feeling that there was absolutely no need to continue to appear holy and maintain acts of righteousness and obedience on god's behalf because he already knew my true heart anyway. I felt that I should just let go of all the devout Christian obedience I was supposed to adhere to.

In these moments of fear about the eternal consequences for leaving my faith I also heard:

"Doesn't the bible say that I have not given a spirit of fear but of love?

Doesn't the bible say that all the law depends on one thing and that is love?

Doesn't the bible say that I AM love?"

What I was learning in that moment of clarity was that if I was that afraid of what my creator might do to punish my unfaithfulness then was what I was encountering really god? Or was what I was encountering indoctrination and generations of being told all about god from an outside source instead of straight from the "horse's mouth" or directly from god's spirit within me.

This principal of having a relationship with god that a child does with a loving parent is relayed in Hebrew 3:5-6, when we are told **Moses related to god as an obedient servant to commands and rules, BUT Christ was faithful not because of his servant hood or obedience, Christ was considered faithful because he was a Son**. We then see the results of relating to the Creator as a son and a beloved relative instead of obedient servants. **This benefit to being a Son as opposed to a servant is referred to as "rest" in chapter 4**. This "rest" from working for god is the same as experiencing the Promised Land, eternal life, and the kingdom of heaven. The kingdom of heaven being the ability to forgive ourselves from shame and guilt through righteousness, the ability to feel like all situations work out for our good through peace of mind, and the ability to enjoy life to the fullest degree in all situations through joy in the Spirit; this is what I refer to as the amazingly easy and good life.

How is this rest obtained, once again by hearing the voice of the spirit and having a soft heart to that voice as is stated in Hebrews 3 & 4. In other words, being easily led by the voice of the spirit within our hearts as opposed to the guidance of spiritual or religious leaders, produces the rest or amazingly easy life that is ours to live. And this softening of hearts and being led by the spirit is not our work to obey as servants who are endangered with being punished for disobedience. This leading by our spirit is given as a free gift to the sons and daughters of humanity who are heirs to all that god is. It is not because we are not good enough that we do not experience this rest and easy abundant life. We do not experience it because we simply do not ask for it as a free gift of grace. (James 4:3).

What I was now seeing was that I had every right to approach my spiritual parent on even more familiar terms than I did to my earthly parents. Jesus advised his followers that if they wanted to experience peace and joy and the ability to forgive, then to approach god as children to a parent not as minions or servants to a master (Matthew 18:3). When I visit my mother's house I put my feet on the couch, raid the refrigerator, and have heart to hearts on a frequent basis. I know that what is hers is mine and what is mine is hers. This is precisely the way it is with our spiritual parent.

If the nagging paranoia of being separated from our source re-enters my heart and grips me with terror, then I remind myself that the idea of being separate from the very source of our existence based on our failure to please it comes from the guidance of flawed human religious leaders, not from the creator himself. We can only know what the creator is truly guiding us to do by listening to the still small voice in our own hearts. I also remember to ask myself, "Can we be separated from the Sun that shines on everything and everyone? Can we escape the wind that is everywhere and blows on everything and everyone? Can we earn to be warmed and lit by the Sun? Can we earn to be cooled by the wind?"

Being separate from god is like saying the Sun shines on a select few but on the vast majority of the undeserving, there is only darkness. The true source of all existence cannot be boxed, taught, or deserved; this is religion. I believe the true source of everything is for everybody and has the same bonded connection with all of existence.

A Still Small Voice

The key now is to acknowledge that automatic connection and cooperate with its gentle and loving promptings that are permanently embedded into our hearts. Some, but not all, of the guiding words I heard while listening to the still small voice in my heart were also confirmed with various scriptures I was led to see with fresh eyes instead of interpreting them the way they had always been fed to me. This fresh interpretation of spiritual principals from the Judeo-Christian scriptures confirmed what I first heard in my heart and truly freed me from all of the handcuffs of the religious legalism and of having to obey as a prisoner does a warden. This spiritual inner guidance opened me up to a totally cost-free, automatic connection that filled me with an ecstatic child-like love of life.

The most liberating truth I was led to as a result of my prayers and tears of desperation was that I was free and clear to follow the spirit's guidance for myself instead of the co-dependent and coddling guidance I was looking to other flawed humans for. Instead of being restricted to what I had to do and was forbidden to do, I was learning more and more that I was free to hear and be led by what my heart was revealing to me as opposed to merely reading printed text that was open to human opinion and ulterior motives. Once I was at least open to being primarily guided by my spirit's guidance, I was able to see and hear more clearly. I began to not only hear the voice of the parenting heart of god through scriptures but also through observing nature, listening to music, watching films, having enlightening conversation with friends, reading inspirational books, or even from other principles found in other religious cultures such as the Buddhism and Hinduism. I was beginning to hear and find the guidance that I was literally crying in anguish about how to enjoy life by becoming willing to hear god from anywhere and everywhere. As a result I discovered that although our Creator does indeed speak though Judeo-Christian scripture, he also speaks and uses everything at his disposal to communicate with us.

Ezekiel 36:26-30 was a key passage along the way in showing me that I could enjoy life on earth by first and foremost listening to my inner voice speaking from within my very own heart as opposed to looking for god's word from other men whom I mistakenly assumed were more spiritual, wiser, and closer to god than I. What I didn't know was that I was just as close to the heart of the creator and had just a special inside relationship with him as everyone I considered closer to god. Oh how I longed for what "they had", each and every time I would listen to a minister speak in a church service. Surely they had a special intimate relationship with the creator, but me, I was merely a peasant desperately doing all the "right things" to become a guest as opposed to a resident in god's house.

An example of hearing god's voice in unlikely places is in the book of Numbers when a man named Balak, the king of Moab, wanted a prophet by the name of Balaam to come to him and speak against the people of Israel. Balaam was known for his accurate prophecies. So Balak offers to pay Balaam big money for his prophecy. Then, as Balaam starts the journey to visit Balak and give him a prophecy for the destruction of Israel, the donkey that Balaam was riding saw an angel blocking their path and stopped dead in its tracks. Balaam proceeded to strike the donkey out of anger until the bible says, god opened the mouth of the donkey and **the donkey spoke to the prophet Balaam** and asked why he was striking him. Then god opened Balaam's spiritual awareness to be able to see the angel that the donkey already saw. The angel told Balaam that it was indeed blocking the donkey because **his journey was not authorized by god.** (Numbers 22:1-34)

I share this paraphrased story because I now see myself as the donkey who can see more clearly my own personal spiritual path instead of the path that men, who are considered a spiritual authority, have set me on. I am merely the donkey that has veered off course in opposition to the commands of kings and prophets but can now freely live based on what I can see for myself. In fact, it is my assumption that everyone is a donkey and can only travel their own spiritual path that will always go against what spiritual authority has for you which will most certainly get you struck with rejection and slander for your rebellion. However, if your goal is to see and hear more clearly the path that the creator has for you, than I dare say it has to be spear-headed by your own personal built-in connection with the source of all that is alive and well within you.

I am now able to live and enjoy myself as a sheep that recognizes that shepherds voice within me and only moves when my shepherd calls as opposed to coming when any other shepherd calls for me from outside of my inner voice. (John 10:27).

I am now more closely identifying with Elijah's experience when he heard a gentle small voice inside of him (I Kings 19:11-13). When I heard that small gentle voice for myself, I began to see and feel that I didn't have to follow Christian tradition and could enjoy life as I followed my own spiritual path.

Although I am still inspired by god's voice through scripture, which is why I quote and reference scripture throughout this book, I now see that scriptures importance is the opposite of what I learned in Christianity. I learned that the printed text of the bible was the authority and everything we heard within us was supposed to be tested by what we read in the bible. I now have experienced that what I hear in my heart is more valid than what I read in the bible because it provides more inspiration and life giving messages within me than merely following traditions. I can cross-reference what I feel speaking to me inside my heart with what I have read in scripture if it adds to the inspiration but the ultimate test is not if I also find it in scripture. The ultimate test for me is if it causes me to love others more. Even the passage in I John 4:1-6 that instructs us to test what we hear, does not instruct us to use bible verses as validation. I John 4:7 advises that the real test of what we hear within us is how well we love others.

As Kramer asked in one of my favorite episodes of Seinfeld, "Now, what does the little man inside you say? See you gotta listen to the little man … The little man knows all" Then George, to whom he was speaking, laments, "My little man is an idiot!" This hilarious scene from the wildly popular TV show has a ton of truth to reveal to us. I now see that each and every one of us has a little man inside which is our spirit or our measure of faith that we are all given (Romans 12:3). That is why this same verse advises us to not think more highly of ourselves than others because we are all just as spiritual as everyone else, we all have the same strength of bond and connection with the creator, Christian or Non-Christian, religious or non-religious, "spiritual" or non-spiritual.

This is the first step in truly loving others or loving our neighbor as we love ourselves. You see our "neighbor" is anyone who is different than us in race, religion, gender, or lifestyle. **If we read and obey scripture but do not love others who are not Christians, who profess no faith, then we have interpreted incorrectly.** If we have heard anything within our heart and do not love others because they are not as spiritual as us and judge them or think lower of them, then we have heard incorrectly.

Being Led By The Spirit

While there are many people who profess faith that genuinely produce love for others and enjoyment in life, this is not only for those who claim a certain faith. This is because faith and spirituality is not exclusive to a limited group of special chosen people who have it in good with god and the disobeyers are left out. No, **each and every one of us has a measure of faith or a little man or a spirit that is intrinsically, innately, and inherently linked, connected, and hooked up with the source of all life aka "The big man".** The little man is the apparatus that the big man uses to translate what he wants us to know and where he wants us to go on our individualized spiritual journeys.

We are not all on the same path. Each of us are on very different paths but our very own little men are our own personal GPS systems to where we are headed. This little man or still small voice is given to all of us to lead us to our destination of loving life and loving one another passionately! All we have to do is be open to everything's potential to speak to us as the donkey did to Balaam and not think more highly of ourselves than we ought because everyone has the same level of potential guidance from this inner voice given to lead us.

If we are to begin living by being led by our spirit then our only duty is to say, as Samuel did, "speak for I am listening" (I Samuel 3:4-11). Then we will be able to recognize when our spirit is guiding us with our built-in GPS system and would feel the most vibrant expression of love for life and one another, which is our ultimate purpose of our spiritual journey. So, let that be our constant expression to our source, "I am listening." "I give you permission to bring willingness to my heart and humility to my mind so that I can hear what you are truly saying." "I give you permission to allow me to see what you are truly showing me especially if it means hearing and seeing different than my strongest beliefs and then be able to love my life and love others as a result."

When we truly love ourselves as the creator loves us then we will know what to do in our lives, we will have the best advisor, the best consigliore to our godfather, the best counselor on a constant basis because we will be led by the spirit of love. We will experience this spirit, which is the source of all that exists, searching the deepest, inner most recesses of our hearts and gently prompting us and teaching us according to our spiritual learning style.

The spirit knows the way in which we will best receive what we need to hear and does not mind putting the medicine we need in with the orange juice that we enjoy. This is how we are led by the spirit, which is the way we are designed to relate to the creator. We are not designed to relate to the creator based on obedience to commands and non-negotiable truths. We are designed to be led by our little man's connection with the source of all that exists and allow it to guide us and teach us in all things. Therefore the spirit that is the invisible source of all things will also personally guide us and be our personal aide and assistant in all things John 14:16-26.

In fact, this is what many believers would refer to as the new covenant in Romans 8:1-17 when we are instructed to be led by the spirit as children would be to their daddy instead of as obedient servants who are condemned based on how they perform rules. This inner guidance will lead us into the Promised Land or this amazingly good life and abundant life that I speak of.

This is the true eternal life that Jesus presented to his followers. I do not believe it was designed to be reserved for the afterlife or that it refers to going to heaven when we physically die. I believe that is a misinterpretation based on our traditional views that are passed down to us when we are taught what the scriptures mean by our well-meaning spiritual caregivers. I believe that the eternal life Jesus speaks of, the promised land Moses speaks of, is intended and designed as an experience and a way in which we live our lives here on earth and it is a feeling of being nourished with milk and honey and a feeling of being raised from the dead and alive with excitement and ecstasy.

Avoiding punishment or wrath in the afterlife was never a part of the plan. The only punishment that I can see is the inability to truly enjoy life and feeling trapped in experiencing suffering here on earth, which everyone experiences, not just "unbelievers". The true good news is that we don't have to live this way anymore. We can love our lives, love our selves, love our existence, love our experiences, and love one another just as passionately as we love our own lives. This only happens when we stop living life according to our wisdom, ability, effort, or agenda and allow our little man to direct our lives and simply ask and acknowledge it in everything (Zechariah 4:6, Prov. 3:5-8). Then we will experience the spirit giving us exactly what we need to live life to the fullest because we have given it permission to search our innermost deepest part of us and give us what it knows we need instead of what we are getting with our own agenda (Romans 8:27, Hebrews 4:12-13, Matthew 6:31-32).

We will see and experience that obedience to the law or what we believe the bible says will indeed kill us inside and we will still experience depression, frustration, and emptiness with merely practicing Christianity. However, being led by our spirit will give us life and we will experience overflowing fullness, overwhelming joy, and an unexplainable but healthy pleasure with ourselves (2 Corinthians 3:1-6). And as an ultimate result we will know how amazingly easy and good life can be because our spirit and our source is expressing itself through us and living for us (Exodus 4:10-12, Matthew 10:19-20, I John 2:27).

The Fruit Of The Spirit

Jesus compares all of humanity to a seed in Matthew 13:1-43 and calls for us to bear fruit in John 15:1-6. This is because we all, as the family of god, are the seeds and have this spirit connection to the Creator, the only difference is which seeds are bearing fruit. I believe many people misinterpret this scripture in Matthew 13 because they believe the seed is the faith of practicing Christianity. Many also misinterpret the scripture in John 15 because they believe that those who do not bear fruit are burned and condemned to hell in the afterlife.

Since all of humanity has been given a spirit connection with the creator and have the potential to activate that spiritual connection, the fruit of the spirit is the defining evidence of that connection. If we claim to have faith but are not producing what is listed as the fruit of the spirit then we are just practicing religion. I have personally witnessed those who claim no faith produce the evidence of an active spirit connection.

The fruit of the spirit is:

Love of others without requirements

Enjoyment in sad situations

Rest in stressful situations

Being kind to the unkind

Being good to those who do bad things

Easily trusting our concerns and areas of past hurts to our spirit's care and control

Being gentle to the un-loveable

And the ability to spiritually check ourselves and see when we need to grow and mature in an unhealthy area of our lives (Galatians 3:22-23).

If we do not bear this fruit as seeds of humanity, then we experience inner suffering in life which is referred to as the "fire" that burns. We know this because the last part of this verse in Galatians informs us that there is no law to obey, no commandments to follow if we are simply loving our lives and loving others just as Jesus informed us when he said **love your neighbor as much as you love yourself, for this covers all of the fruit of the spirit and there is no law or religion for this**. Again we see that the true test of if we are connecting with god is NOT how well we obey scripture but how well we love others just like it is mentioned in I John 4:7

Our only requirement then is, not to convert to any teaching, but to be aware we have a seed or spirit that we share with all of humanity, follow the guidance and wisdom that lies within that seed as a still small voice, then we will produce the full ecstatic enjoyment of life that is to be freely given to others. This experience of truly loving others will cause us to feel and sense an even more exuberant celebration where we feel rich on the inside and feel like jumping and leaping with endless gratitude, and just as the crippled man who was healed, we'll be able to easily move forward in life and walk again.

The seed or spirit that we all possess has the untapped potential and possibility to bear this fruit of love without requirements and this is not only reserved for Christians or those who profess a particular faith.

The only requirement to producing fruit here on Earth is having the seed or spirit that is given to each and every one of us according to Romans 12:3. This is why I believe we can see some who do not profess a certain faith or practice any religion have such a peace and joy about them and some people we meet who profess faith are in turmoil and strife, because they are either producing or not producing the fruit of loving others **through first loving themselves.**

This then is the key: the reason why Jesus instructs us to love others as much **as we love ourselves is because it is imperative that we love ourselves first**. How do we love ourselves first? We love ourselves first by feeling about our existence and individual personality the same way god feels about our existence and individual personality. I John 4:19 lets us know that **we can only love because he first loves us. So we must first experience the passion that god really feels about us.**

God Is Love

How we reach this experience of feeling what the creator feels towards us is asking for an awareness of vibrant admiration and healing love towards ourselves, then releasing that love to our fellow humans that we share the planet with. (Luke 10:25-28)

The real issue of why we don't feel this love for ourselves and others is due to what our life experiences have falsely communicated to us instead of what our creator and the source of all life actually feels towards us at all times. For instance, if we experience something that makes us feel worthless and unimportant, then we subconsciously tell ourselves we are worthless and unimportant. However, our source and originator of life and existence feels as if we are the most important person in the world. How we may feel if the president of the US came to visit our home, or if the CEO of the company we work for wanted to hang out with us. Think of wealthiest, most affluent person you admire like a Bill Gates or maybe even a unifying figure like Pope Francis or the Dali Lama and they just wanted to get to know you personally and talk to you and pay attention to you and be your personal friend and looked at you as an equal; This is precisely how the creator feels about us constantly: honored, proud, and with strong admiration.

You see, the number one problem in the world is not that we are sinners, wicked, or evil. The number one problem is that we do not know our worth, we are unaware of how valuable and worthy of being treasured and cherished we are. It is lack of knowledge why we perish or why we suffer in life and burn with desire for things we can't seem to have (Hosea 4:6). It is not the lack of knowledge of information but the lack of knowledge of who we are and of our full worth. We do not know that we are literally priceless.

Do you remember those Master Card commercials? They listed the price of various items that were being purchased but the last part said something like, "The look on her face when....priceless": This is what you mean to your source, designer, and creator. This why we have not yet learned to love one another passionately, this is why we have not learned to love our very own selves passionately.

Although we are taught from the current interpretation of scripture that the first thing we should know is that we are born sinners and need to repent, I humbly offer that we re-read the scriptures with love in mind, not according to traditional doctrine, because the creator does not love teachings or doctrines more than he loves you and I. For it is the "kindness of God that leads to repentance" (Romans 2:4) and repentance is not what we traditionally have been taught it is. It is not thinking we are underserving and being fearful of the consequences, so we beg and plead for god to have mercy upon us. God wants mercy for us more than we desire it for ourselves therefore we don't have to beg for it. In fact, god is mercy by the very definition and expression of the term and that is the only thing he knows how to do. All he can produce from his character is constant freedom from holding grudges.

The origin of the word repent is a change in perspective, it has nothing to do with feeling sorry or ashamed or guilty. The origin of the word actual means an alteration in perspective without shame. In fact, according to Romans, true repentance occurs with an awareness of the kindness god feels towards us. Therefore, "Getting it right" is not what the creator had in mind for us. We are not designed to be "right" in the argument with society about morality or universal truth. I have come to find, through my very own love encounter with the creator that he is not concerned with whether we know the "truth" as far as teachings go. I have come to find that the creator is only concerned with us and whether we know how he truly, genuinely feels towards us; just like the prodigal son did not know how his father really felt about him while he was wallowing with hogs. The prodigal son was pleasantly surprised that his father actually wanted to throw him a party because of how elated the father was to see him. Therefore our only requirement is not feeling shame and guilt and sorrow about our sins but our only requirement is knowing how kindly god feels towards us, this and only this will cause us to easily let go of all unhealthy behavior that causes our own suffering, not shame and guilt and holding grudges against ourselves and others.

I have come to feel and experience that the creator thinks more highly of us than all of the angels in heaven and all of the Suns, Moons, and Stars in all of the galaxies. If we were to be able to see all of the celestial beings in all of their wonder, amazement, and glory we would see how beautiful they are and how vital they are to the planets in providing essential energy that the universe and life forms need to exist. Yet we are more beautiful, wonderful, amazing, and glorified than all the celestial beings in the creator's eyes. We are his most prized possession! You and I are the masterpiece that he is most proud of. We are his most premiere and exclusive work for we are placed higher than the angels and all things that are placed in our hands for us to rule and master. We are only a little lower than the creator himself in the hierarchy of existence (Psalm 8:3-8, Psalm 82:6). This means that we are also creators of our own world, our own lives, and we literally have superhuman powers to create for ourselves the desires of our heart with a genuine love for others.

This love of others can happen only when we feel about ourselves the same that the creator feels about us; thrilled and overjoyed, special and exhilarating, warm and fuzzy all over, the same way we feel towards our children in their most innocent and cutest moments. The only difference is that the creator feels this to the highest, most infinite, never ending level and is not limited by condition of human performance. Therefore, this is the way he feels about us ALL THE TIME!!!. Nothing we can do can shake or break this sheer overwhelming celebration that the creator feels about us (Romans 8:38-39). You are sooooooo loved and adored and honored as an immaculate offspring of the creator with all of his DNA and energy coursing and rushing through your veins and pumping in your heart. This we know because God is literally Love itself, so it is all he does to perfection.

On top of all of this we can know that we are right with god or have a special favored relationship with god, not because we have admitted and relented to our evil nature and repented from our despicable behavior, but because we are only following love as the standard because ALL of the law and the prophets, all obedience to god depends on love alone, not on our behavior or having the right theology. All obedience to god's word and will is founded in love. (Matthew 7:1-12, Matthew 22:34-40,

Mark 12:28-34, Luke 10:25-37, I John 4:1-21, Ephesians 3:14-20)

If we have wondered how god really and truly is in his essence and relationship with humanity, it is not that god is judgment of sin, it is not that god is the great disciplinarian, or god is so righteous that he cannot stand to be with wicked humanity. No, I have experienced and tasted that god is pure, raw, uncut, unedited, undiluted, unadulterated, exhilarating, life-giving love.

Imagine if your parents only talked to you or approached you when you messed up and did something wrong and were only concerned with correcting your behavior. That is not love. True correction through unconditional love is building a strong love bond with our children so that they know how special they are to us. True discipline is gentle and kind instruction and accountability based on that special loving bond. It is not, "you better do things my way or else", it is "sweetheart the best way to go about that is this way and if you do it the other way you will not get your desired results". God's love gently instructs us and lets us know that he literally has our very best interest in mind and gently prompts us to follow our hearts; where he guides and directs us from.

If we wonder what loving the creator with all our heart means, it is not our un-dying allegiance, or our devout righteousness. We can relax and take comfort in the fact that that the creator first loved us. Therefore it is not our feeble, swaying love and devotion that the creator desires. The creator only desires us to know how much it first wildly and ecstatically loves us. (I John 4:19). This is the "first things first" of all religion and all worship to god; accept, receive, feel, and know the fullness of the creator's hysteric love for you and I.

How then do we know what exactly this love looks like? Does it look like the traditional image of god we have; that judges the living and the dead and will punish sin?

If god is indeed love, then we have to understand the definition of love which is the definition of god, not in vocabulary but in experience. Whatever love is, god is.

Love is long patience when someone wrongs us

Love is kindness and thoughtfulness

Love is not jealous, controlling, or manipulative love is understanding

Love is not argumentative and defensive, love is gentle and humble

Love is not rude or impolite, love is polite and courteous

Love does not seek its own way

Love is not overly sensitive or easily angered it does not take into account offenses, so love is easily and overly forgiving

Love does not take pleasure in mistreatment, so love treats us better than we treat ourselves

Love can tolerate any evil or wrong doing that exists, so love completely and overly covers all the wrong that can be done

Love looks for the best in everything and everyone

Love hopes the best about everything and everyone

Love never disappoints or breaks promises (I Corinthians 13:1-13)

If love is all of these things then why do we not define our creator in these terms when we say that god is love? You see we can be looked at as the most spiritual person or the closest to god based on how we minister, how holy we behave, how right our teachings are but none of any of that means a penny if we have not experienced this kind of love and can freely give this kind of love away. **If love does not keep account of wrong doing, if love covers all of our mistakes and bad decisions, if loves does not seek its own way, if love is polite and overly forgiving then this is all of who god is**, not what god does or how god behaves, but it is who god is. The experience of these life-giving encounters with love is experiencing god.

Part 2
For those seeking a spiritual experience without religion

The source of all life and existence in all of the Universe is what we humans who speak the English language, refer to as god. The English version of the word go(o)d actually comes from a variation of the word good and the idea of a personality who is the initiator of good, and the (d)evil being the personality who is the initiator of evil. So to my knowledge, in the English language we define god as the Ultimate Good and the devil as the Ultimate Evil since their English names came from the characteristics they represented. This is precisely the reason why what we call either energy does not matter. Many religious groups may get hung up on what we should call god, when the word g-o-d is simply the English way of saying, the personality who initiates good.

This idea of mystical entities representing certain characteristics comes from ancient cultures that first enacted an organized system of philosophies that were told through mythological stories and caricatures. To my knowledge, one of the first cultures to originate the idea of organizing philosophies of worship towards mystical unseen entities was the Egyptians who used mystical, mythological caricatures to embody principles. For instance, Jesus being born on December 25th, being killed and then raising from the dead is the characteristic given to a deified person that represents the shortest amount of time the actual Sun takes to set and rise after the Winter Solstice around December 25th. Ancient cultures celebrated this day because winter was over and spring was on the way and worshipped the Sun, or as we call it the Son, for winning over the darkness of winter. This being the case, I do believe in an actual historical person named Jesus who was a Jewish Rabbi but do not believe many of the mythological characteristics given to him through the centuries.

I also believe that the reason why Christian philosophies such as virgin births, resurrections from death, afterlife, blessings from pleasing the gods, or curses from upsetting the gods are also sacred Christian principles is because they were actually first communicated by ancient Egyptians then adapted by early Christian followers from Egyptian mythological stories. The reason for this adaptation of religious beliefs from mythological stories is because Egypt historically enslaved Hebrew slaves and infused their belief systems with originally Egyptian principles. Jewish people then passed these original Egyptian ideas through their religious writings in scripture and onto Christianity who is the offshoot of Hebrew Judaism.

One of the key components of the power of slavery is to strip an original culture's identity of their original religious ideas and essentially brainwash them into taking on the enslaving cultures principles. We see the same in the time of the New Testament with Hebrews who lived in Judea and Galilee under Roman colonialism. It was during this time that Herod ordered the Temple in Jerusalem to be reconstructed, where the Jewish people worshipped prior to Roman colonialism. He also completely transformed their land and capital city of Jerusalem as he installed a Greek administration as well as Roman institutions and customs that were in violation of the Jews own sacred traditions of the Torah. With this came a transformation and overhaul of their religious beliefs that now included Greek and Roman myths such as pleasing or upsetting the gods to gain blessings and avert curses. This is the context in which the early Christians did not fully take on the new teaching of the historical Rabbi Jesus that the Kingdom of heaven is not a place you go to in the afterlife for how you please god. The early Christians were under the religious culture of the times where they were taught to strictly obey the Old Testament in order to please the Creator. However, this was the way of worshipping that Jesus came to reform with his new teaching of the Kingdom of heaven is within you and love your neighbor as yourself.

Although Greeks and Romans believed in polytheism, Jewish culture interpreted the pleasing of gods into monotheistic traditions and now taught that pleasing god through scared religious traditions or upsetting him to deserve punishment for failure to follow those traditions is the way to relate to the source of all existence. This limited view became prevalent and dominant and is now how we have thought of and worshipped the source or creator, when how we do so has indeed, unbeknownst to us, been tainted and polluted with mere human traditions that the creator has zero concern or demand for.

Therefore, let us not so much focus on calling the all-encompassing force of love and good in the Universe g-o-d because it invokes a limited image that does a grave disservice to the true nature of the source of all that exists. When anyone says g-o-d most people immediately see the Caucasian male who is painted atop the Sistine Chapel, which is a mere fictional animation. They also mostly imagine a vengeful and angry character who punishes wrongdoing and is reluctant to bless humanity because of their sinful nature that he installed into their biological hard drive to function that way. The only way to deserve or earn his blessings then is to plead and beg forgiveness from your evil nature and follow all of his commands as Lord over your life. The penalty for failing to do this is torture through being burned without end.

The same is true of Jesus who most people imagine as a long haired peaceful European hippie, also a fictional animation, whose birth is celebrated December 25th, was born of a virgin, performed miracles, came to overthrow a governmental dictatorship, was killed in the process, and rose again three days later. It may surprise you to know as it did me when I first discovered that these same exact details of Jesus' biography are not exclusive to Jesus of Nazareth but also mythological caricatures that predate Jesus thousands of years, such as Horus, Mithras, Krishna, and Dionysus. What does this mean? To me it means that these sacred untouchable biographical details that are intended to prove Jesus' deity also were adapted and lifted from previous culture's deities and savior's so it is hard for me to believe that these details we now assert solely to Jesus as truth. The Jesus that lived and walked the earth has nothing to do with the myths we have psychologically inherited from the power of traditional stories passed down from generation to generation. So what or who is god really? I believe god is the English name we have traditionally inherited as the deified character that represents good on earth but that the true nature and function of what we call god is actually the source of all existence in the entire Universe. How then should humanity relate to the source of not only our human existence on the planet earth but all of existence in all the Universe?

As of now we may view god religiously. We may view god according to what we have heard from our spiritual care givers who have passed down a message and reputation about god that flawed men, who may or may not have had a selfish agenda have propagated. While I acknowledge these statements sounds blasphemous and offensive, I sincerely apologize to anyone offended because my true intention is to allow everyone from the non-religious to the religious to have full access to their connection with the source from whence we come. This connection cannot be forced or initiated by humanity in any way. In fact, this connection exists for every single one of us in non-religious terms that do not require any piety or obedience on our part. The power that religion has had for so long has been the power of fear. I truly have experienced that anything we do because we are deathly afraid of the consequences is not as genuine of an experience as we may believe. At a crucial point deep into my own experience with god, I realized that the original motivation for my commitment to serve god as a Christian was because I did not want to go to hell. Then as I went deeper into my commitment to serve god I did not want to be "left behind" in the rapture because I believed we were living in the end times before Christ returned to earth to rescue the faithful and destroy the wicked. Therefore, my main reason for my devout service and commitment was fear.

This is a message and story I wanted to share and make relatable to everyone and every kind of special and precious human being: Every single life that exists, has ever existed, and ever will, including yours, is to be cherished and treasured as the most valuable prize of all!

Knowing and feeling this cherishing and valuing of your life and the lives of everyone is the beginning to falling deeply in love with life and was the beginning to my amazing discovery that life is meant to be a precious gift.

With that being said we all can experience an ecstatic love of life and find meaning for our existence without following any religious traditions because our lives have equal value regardless of religious performances.

Now the question becomes how do we fully enjoy life if we are not religious or do not practice any faith. I have found an overwhelming enjoyment of life by first of all placing the highest value on my life as precious and treasured. I now view my existence and personal experiences as cherished gifts that are meant to benefit me. I then became aware that I did not need any outside wisdom to guide me on my life's journey. I realize that all wisdom that gives us the ability and skill to live a life full of enjoyment is already within us. We do not have a need to read self-help books and go to inspirational seminars to find the inspiring messages that we need to guide us to our true destiny. We need look no further than within our own hearts for the words we need to guide us to self-fulfillment in life. Each and every one of us are designed with an inner light that guides us with a whisper. We only need to pause our hectic lives and acknowledge it on a daily basis for its individual guidance of our life's evolution into our higher selves, which is unconditional love of life and others. Our goal in life then becomes not making it to heaven when we die but being the healthiest happiest human we can be. Life then becomes not about what we accomplish through what we do but being who we truly are through our cooperation with our inner awareness. Life is not a matter of doing the right things but it is a matter of seeing the right things through our perspective and as a result living out our highest selves because we can now clearly see where we going. We are merely a new perspective away from fully loving our lives as healthy and happy beings and evolving into our true nature of love.

In order to become healthier humans we must know that the healthiest antidote to human suffering is unity and unconditional love and the cause of all human suffering is hate and division. To truly care for ourselves and rid our lives of unnecessary suffering through the experience of any negative emotion when we encounter a negative situation we must learn to treat ourselves as opposed to looking for treatment outside of ourselves. The cure that lies within us is the super human ability to love where there is hate.

While our negative life experiences has taught us to feel hate through the emotions of anger and depression we must realize that entertaining feelings of negative emotions makes us sicker and unhealthy humans. We can know we are not healthy in our human souls by how much we enjoy life. If we barely enjoy our lives then we have indeed been feeding ourselves the poison of bad emotions and unnecessarily entertaining them. Whenever we feel any negative emotion we can know that it is a sign that we don't have to feed into it and can apply the cure to ourselves in order to fully enjoy life. Feeling positive emotions is not a matter of what we are supposed to do because it is right. Feeling and entertaining positive emotions is more so a matter of being the cure for feeling unhealthy as human beings whenever we are unhappy. Our happiness levels is the gauge to how healthy we are and whenever we feel unhappy and unhealthy with negative emotions we can give permission to our inherent positive emotions to fill our hearts and cure of us the negative emotion that we suffer from.

If we are concerned and worried we can activate peace of mind. If we are angry and frustrated we can activate forgiveness. If we are depressed we can activate joy. If we are afraid to be ourselves because we care about what people think about us then we can activate self-love. If we judge others and are view anyone lower than we view and value ourselves, if we think we are better than anyone else then we can activate love for others. These positive emotions are not a mystical intangible myth but are intimately apart of our nature and human DNA. As we learn to activate these positive emotions and beliefs about ourselves we will discover a truly ecstatic love of life and freedom from suffering because we are taking the best medicine to live the healthiest life we can live by loving ourselves and others during negative experiences.

Made in the USA
Charleston, SC
02 April 2016